VOICE RECOGNITION

James **Byrne** is editor of *The Wolf*, a leading poetry magazine. Born in 1977, he lives in London. He co-founded New Blood, an event featuring young poets in London. Currently, he is co-editing a *Collected Poems* of Hope Mirrlees. His first book, *Passages of Time*, was published by Flipped Eye in 2003, and his second collection, *Blood/Sugar*, by Arc in 2009.

Clare Pollard was born in Bolton in 1978 and currently lives in East London. She has published three collections with Bloodaxe, *The Heavy-Petting Zoo* (1998), *Bedtime* (2002) and *Look, Clare! Look!* (2005), with her fourth due from Bloodaxe in 2011. Her first play *The Weather* (Faber, 2004) premièred at the Royal Court Theatre. She works as an editor, broadcaster and teacher. Her recent documentary for radio, 'My Male Muse (2007), was a Radio 4 Pick of the Year, and she is a Royal Literary Fund Literary Fellow at Essex University.

VOICE RECOGNITION

21 POETS FOR THE 21ST CENTURY

EDITED BY
JAMES BYRNE & CLARE POLLARD

BLOODAXE BOOKS

ISBN: 978 1 85224 838 3

First published 2009 by
Bloodaxe Books Ltd,
Highgreen,
Tarset,
Northumberland NE48 1RP.

Second impression 2010.

www.bloodaxebooks.com
For further information about Bloodaxe titles
please visit our website or write to
the above address for a catalogue.

Supported by
**ARTS COUNCIL
ENGLAND**

Cover design: Neil Astley & Pamela Robertson-Pearce

Printed in Great Britain by
Bell & Bain Limited, Glasgow, Scotland.

CONTENTS

James Womack (*b.* 1979)

INTRODUCTION

Welcome to *Voice Recognition* – an anthology that brings together 21 of the best young poets who have yet to publish a full collection. This book arrives at a particularly important moment for poetry in Britain and Ireland, where the presence of young poets is beginning to revitalise the scene.

For many years the poetry world has belonged to older writers. Few young poets were published and fewer were nominated for the major prizes. An invitation to a poetry reading conjured thoughts of warm white wine in a pokey bookshop or plodding recitals in a half empty village hall. Being a poet was uncool. The average poetry reader, we were told, was retired, and young people weren't interested, preferring to get their poetic fix from song lyrics. For us, it sometimes felt as though poetry had lost its energy and was becoming stagnant. On the publication of this book we realise that, although it is vital that poetry's more seasoned voices must continue to flourish and are justly celebrated, a literature without young voices is often one without young readers, and has little future.

Over the last few years there has been a surge of interest in young poets. The main reason for this seems to be that support for emerging voices has increased exponentially. Once being a new poet was a lonely business, which involved years of posting off new work to magazines, only to receive rejection slips a year later. Now opportunities to workshop, perform and publish have boomed. In fact, there are more avenues to gain attention as a young writer than at any time before.

For poets under 18, the Foyle Young Poet of the Year Award has generated an increasing buzz, and launched a talented group of teenage writers. Recently it helped to spawn an exciting e-zine for poets under 30, *Pomegranate*. Also representing the under-30s, the Eric Gregory Award remains the principal accolade for new poets. In recent years the announcement of Gregory winners has become a central event in the poetry calendar, followed by a packed reading and poems showcased in *Magma* magazine. In this book, we've included half a dozen recent recipients of the 'Gregory' – though a good many here are still eligible so we'd expect the count to rise. Elsewhere, projects like the *Generation Txt* book and tour have offered a fresh survey of young poets writing in the Britain. Spread the Word has launched its *Complete Works* scheme to support writers from black and Asian backgrounds and the New Writing Partnership has offered major support for new work.

Alongside this, poetry pamphlets have become increasingly significant and have boosted the profile of important new voices who may not yet be ready for a full collection but deserve to be read more widely. Pamphlets by new and emerging poets are increasing in number every year and boosted by initiatives such as the Poetry Book Society Pamphlet Choice and the Michael Marks Awards for Poetry Pamphlets. For many young poets, pamphlets have become a clear stepping-stone to publishing a full collection. Reacting to this, for the first time in its 80-year history, Faber & Faber have now introduced a pamphlet series that will publish some of the best new British poets, five of whom are included in this anthology. This comes after two and a half years of the tall-lighthouse 'Pilot' project, edited by Roddy Lumsden – which has produced debuts from many leading UK poets under 30, including five featured here – and numerous publications by small presses such as Pighog and Smiths Knoll.

Young poets are being recognised in less obvious places too – in clubs, in theatres, at music festivals, in schools. They are now a part of major poetry festivals, where once they were a token programming gesture. Indeed, throughout Britain and Ireland young poets have become a key fixture at live events, many of which are run by their contemporaries. As the credit crunch exposes the superficiality of many of the last decade's bloated, corporate values, there is a young generation who seem to hungering for the authentic and DIY. Embracing this approach, new poet-promoters are setting up their own nights like the spoken word event *14 Hour*, the *Openned* series at The Foundry, both of these in London, and magazines like *Stop/ Sharpening/ Your/ Knives* from Norwich. A particular hub of this activity appears to be London, where many of the poets in this anthology are based – after years of other regions being prominent, there seems a real shift back to the capital, which is becoming a magnet for poets all over the country.

Outside of poetry gigs, the first generation to benefit from studying Creative Writing has also emerged. Almost every university going seems to have a poetry course, which is frequently backed by a renowned faculty. In the graduate workshop setting, poets are able to improve as technicians of poems and, more importantly, develop a relationship with student-poets of their own generation. Getting this kind of feedback is essential and often hard to find outside of the classroom. But if there is main criticism of the MA (and some non-academic poetry workshops can be included in this), it is that they can encourage conformities of style. Many proficient young poets we have looked at for inclusion ultimately fell away because they had a distinctly similar way of behaving in a poem. In the most obvious cases, obedience tended to prevail over original thought. It is no coincidence that many of the same-sounding, low-stake, well-mannered (but going nowhere) poems we read whilst putting together this anthology were from poets who had recently come along the MA conveyor-belt. However, there is no doubt that for those with natural talent, the combination of mentoring, feedback and opportunities supplied by these courses have made a huge difference to the quality and confidence of their work. The most exceptional poets, of any age, tend to be those who are able to fine-tune their creative instincts beyond the immediacy of study, supervision or curriculum. In *Voice Recognition* we've tried to avoid any poets who conform to archetypes of academic orderliness (though many of our poets have benefited a great deal from graduate study), preferring those who have range, dare and vitality. The poets included in this book are able to react in a number of different ways – but always imaginatively – to what Alvarez termed 'the quick of experience'.

*　　*　　*

2009 has been a year of unprecedented attention for young poets. It began in January when Jen Hadfield received the T.S. Eliot Prize – the UK's single most important award for a poet. Jen, at 30 years of age, became the youngest recipient in the history of the award by some margin. Young poets in Britain and Ireland have since been in an ever-widening spotlight – one example of this was a 17-poet feature entitled 'Young British Poets', edited by Todd Swift for *The Manhattan Review*. For us, there seems no better time to draw on the richness of talent available and to introduce an anthology that encapsulates the best of a generation of poets under 35. Our main task in assembling *Voice Recognition* was simple: to showcase poetry's new stars.

There are said to be over 250 poetry magazines in the UK as well as thousands of e-zines, all publishing 'new writing'. Between us we have attended hundreds of poetry nights and read stacks of pamphlets. Gratefully, we received a bounty of recommendations from other poets, poetry organisations and university lecturers, chasing up tips from every relevant contact we had. Hundreds of poets fitted our catchments of age and publication history, and narrowing the pool was difficult – partly because, in our case, there were few useful templates.

In British poetry the idea of what constitutes 'the new' has long been fought over and recent generational markers (see the New and Next Generation lists) have often been reductive. Ezra Pound famously urged us to 'make it new', but who decides what it means to write new poetry today and what does the new sound like? What makes young poets writing early in this century different from previous generations? These questions were foremost in our mind when shortlisting poets for this anthology.

For us, leading new poets should represent progress, daring, originality and (where possible) an extension of the poetic tradition. In our selection, we sought a healthy approach to diversity – we agreed early on that any mapping we made of British and Irish poets under 35 must include a range of styles. We believe that there are many ways to make a good poem and that young poets shouldn't all sound too alike. Throughout *Voice Recognition* there are meaningful explorations of relationships between page and performance, modernist and post-modern, experimental and avant-garde. Too often in the recent past poetries have stood against one other, whispering in their cliques. This seems only to seal poetry off as a bickering art, discouraging it even further from achieving a deserved and larger readership. The emerging generation of poets in Britain and Ireland have a chance to change this.

Among previous anthologies that had sought to define newness, we were influenced by *The New Poetry*, edited by Alvarez and first published by Penguin in 1962. It was a landmark anthology that scrutinised the island-bound fustiness of the Movement and championed key American poets, especially when Anne Sexton and Sylvia Plath were added to the updated 1966 edition. In Alvarez's excellent introduction, entitled 'The New Poetry, *or* Beyond the Gentility Principle', he extends Pound's dictum by declaring that 'the great moderns experimented not just to make it new formally, but to open poetry up to new areas of experience'. Technique is not enough. Talent must be fuelled by the experience of a life outside of the poems. The best new work being written today must have something to say for itself beyond a mere recounting of anecdotes or minor stagings of epiphany. Many of the poets in this book have benefited from immersing themselves in the creative stimuli that can be found through travel, translation or through a broad appreciation of visual art. They appear able to harvest new ideas at every step in their development, drawing from everyday, but also novelties of experience, in a way that corresponds to Rilke's advice in his *Letters to a Young Poet*:

> It takes a great, fully ripened power to create something individual where good, even glorious, traditions exist in abundance. So rescue yourself from these general themes and write about what your everyday life offers you; describe your sorrows and desires.

Throughout our selection, we sought out those poets who escaped "general themes" and addressed the particularity of being alive now. Though some of the poems here reveal a profound regard for historical figures or events, we were keen to find poets who speak in distinctively 21st-century voices. Consequently, our selection features poetry that confirms a deep fascination with the world as it is today, and reacts by risking new territory.

* * *

So, finally, what territories do these poets explore? All share an ability (rare in poetry) to give something of themselves away – neither cheaply or freely – when opening up the experience of the poem to the reader. This may extend from a wide appreciation of the 'confessional' American poets, though it also seems to derive from an increased awareness of how to deliver a poem to an audience. To quote Kate Potts' poem 'Galatea / *Pygmalion*, Sunday morning', they 'Broadcast the nerve.' Take the edgy narratives of Emily Berry, whose poem 'The Incredible History of Patient M.' concludes:

> The Doctor bites and leaves a mark
> like the fossil of a sprung jaw.
> He slapped my face with his penis.
>
> To get you going, he said. My heart is now
> on red alert, apparently. *If it stops*,
> he reminds me, *you're dead*.

Throughout this book there are poems that interpret richly contrasting mythologies, from Jack Underwood's animal poems to Colm O'Shea's blackly comic 'The Frog Prince', which reworks the fairytale motif into a dark parody of male sexuality:

> *Crrroak*
> I know what the princess dreams –
> her pillow is slick with my toxins.

This contrasts well with poems elsewhere that extend the power of personal mythology by turning to family. Sandeep Parmar catalogues her mother's life in the poem 'Archive for a Daughter', which begins:

> November 1972, Derby
>
>> A dance card embalmed in sweat.
>>> Her ruthless curve of palm
>> mowing the carpet into sheaves before a gas fire.
>
> Liquidescent virgin in a purple dress.

Many of these writers take the "identity politics" of 90s poetry into fresher, more unexpected places, refusing to bow to stereotypes.

Look at Jay Bernard's 'At last we are alone', in which she boldly takes on the voice of a young skinhead who chased her father down the street. Or in Sarah Jackson's backpacking poem 'The Instant of My Death', where she recalls:

> I saw a thin boy in red flannel squat between two dhabas;
>
> a black-eyed bean, slipped-in between two crags, he was so small
> that I almost missed him, until he turned, gap-toothed, and shot me
>
> with a toy gun.

These are also poets fully immersed in a globalised world, who display a commanding filmic sensibility for depicting place, from Jonathan Morley's fascinating interpretation of the Church of Saint Francis, Porto, to Siddhartha Bose's hauntingly elegiac 'Animal City'; a frenetic psychogeographical journey through Mumbai (written a year before the bombings) where:

> ...a thousand gods
> Jostle like men hanging outta late-evening suburban trains,
> Rowdy, brutal, bleeding.

Emily Berry's 'I♥NY' asks an important question for this generation brought up in a time of 'casino capitalism': 'And guilt, / where is that sold?' This questioning of the modern world runs through many of the poems here, as in Ailbhe Darcy's dazzling 'Panopticon' – in which sees her and her father 'Up to our pits in Sunday papers' and exposed to the 'black crawly crawly Darfur fly, man / on a leash, girl with burns, crumpled machinery' – through Joe Dunthorne's take on baby-boomer values in 'A Disastrous Campaign in Bohemia' and Amy Blakemore's dry critique of city boys, 'Making Money'. In 'Crash', Annie Katchinska brilliantly parodies the language of advertising:

> If you got the money buy berries, porridge, bulgur wheat,
> this exotic polysyllabic lettuce that actually *consumes fat inside you*
> or if not, percentages, 3%, 1%, 0%, or traffic light colours.
> Sooper-dooper. Nothing you couldn't work out with a piece of paper
> and a brain and some time but never mind this is prettier.
> This is Comic Sans. This is louder. Come, come.

This is a world where relationships are bought and sold, as in Adam O'Riordan's 'Silver Lake', whose speaker addresses a friend:

> I remember you saying you could order, as if from a menu.
> How the oiled girls lined up to meet-n-greet you.

James Womack's arresting opening line in 'Young Romance' counters a world reduced to porn: 'Let us leave for a moment the bukkake-faced virgin, Our Lady of the pulp-magazine, and look instead into her sunglasses.' This is wittily recontextualised by Miriam Gamble in 'On Fancying American Film Stars' where she remembers how we have existed 'in the bubble of our making, our souls glistening like celluloid'.

But these poets also show poetry to be a powerful antidote to the daily drone of advertising and political propaganda. In an era in which we must quickly understand our impact on this planet, this anthology contains many poets who make us consider the implications of our damage to the natural world, as in Mark Leech's muscular evocations of the Cotswolds, or Toby Martinez de las Rivas' warning:

> Godcundnes is in the world:
> don't turn away from it. Don't turn away,
>   as the kingfisher escapes the river
> with its beakful of silver elvers,
>   and the wren its thorny custody
> in a flash of wings and black underbelly.

All 21 poets are active readers/performers of their own poems and it should not be underestimated how valuable this is to their creative process. In some cases there is an emphasis placed entertaining the audience which means that these poems are often full of both intelligence and humour – as in Ahren Warner's answer to Auden in ' "About suffering they were never wrong, The Old Masters" ', which begins:

> Though, when it comes to breasts, it's a different story.
> Cranach, for example, never seems to have progressed
> beyond his pubescent attempts at apprenticeship;
>
> tennis balls sewn to a pillow of hay, fingers coming
> to terms with the concept of foreplay.

Perhaps most importantly, all of these poets appear guided by a magpie-like ability to tightly grasp any number of worthy ideas for good writing. We believe many of the poems in *Voice Recognition* confirm that, as a young writer, it is not always necessary to stick to one voice; it is often better to risk a multiplicity of styles, and to find the voice appropriate to every poem. Although their writing will inevitably grow, here are poets who already display sound judgements in their own creative process, partly because of a willingness to wait for the right image, or (as Virginia Woolf described in *A Room of One's Own*) to wait for the 'sudden conglomeration of an idea at the end of one's line'. The resulting poems here make up a selection that continues to excite us as editors, but also as poetry readers. We hope this book will be seen as a collection of poems that is able to appeal to both poetry's newcomers and its existing readers. We think there is enough of the cake for everyone.

Compiling this anthology has been a welcome chance for both of us to survey the scene and how it encourages the young poet in Britain. There is an abundance of strong writing out there, particularly by poets who are under 35. We hope this anthology improves each poet's chances of publishing a full collection. These are writers we back all the way, who are capable of greatness. With poetry at such an exciting juncture in Britain and Ireland, we're glad that Bloodaxe recognised the importance of seizing this moment when they commissioned us to compile this anthology. It has been a natural relationship to be working with Neil Astley on bringing *Voice Recognition* into print, as Bloodaxe, more so than any other publisher in Britain, have supported young poets over the last 30 years. We hope this anthology matters enough to readers of all generations and will stand up well over time.

JAMES BYRNE
CLARE POLLARD
London, 2009

ACKNOWLEDGEMENTS

Acknowledgements are due to the following publishers and presses who have published work by various poets included in this anthology in pamphlets mentioned in the biographical notes: Faber & Faber Ltd, Flarestack, Les Figues, Perdika, Pighog, Piper's Ash, tall-lighthouse, and the Wordsworth Trust. Thanks are also due to the editors of the many poetry magazines in which some of these poems, or earlier versions of them, first appeared.

Also, thanks to the Fielding Programme, Foyle Young Poet of the Year, Nathan Hamilton, Happenstance Press, Roddy Lumsden, Poet in the City, The Poetry Society, The Poetry Trust, George Szirtes, George Ttoouli and faculty from the many universities who provided recommendations.

For the author photographs, thanks are due to Neil Astley (Jay Bernard), Peter Barry (Emily Berry), Alex Surguladze (Amy Blakemore), Athanasios Zacharopoulos (Siddhartha Bose), Conor Friel (Ailbhe Darcy), Angus Muir (Joe Dunthorne), Paul Maddern (Miriam Gamble), Paul Radburn (Sarah Jackson), Oleg Katchinski (Annie Katchinska), Claire Leech (Mark Leech), Simona Noli (Toby Martinez de las Rivas), Kris Connolly (Jonathan Morley), the Society of Authors and Adrian Pope (Adam O'Riordan), Colm O'Shea (Colm O'Shea), James Byrne (Sandeep Parmar), Jake Moulson (Heather Phillipson), Will Strange (Kate Potts), Phoebe Bullock (Sophie Robinson), Hannah Bagshaw (Jack Underwood), Nathan Penlington (Ahren Warner) and Ben Womack (James Womack).

JAY BERNARD

Jay Bernard was born in London in 1988, and now studies at Oxford. She won the Respect Slam in 2004 and has gone on to read poetry on radio programmes such as *The Verb* and the *Today Programme*, and at venues from Shakespeare's Globe to the Vienna Lit festival. Jay has been commissioned by the Royal Opera House to write a libretto based on *A Rake's Progress* by William Hogarth. She is a DJ for the Poetry Society and podcasts regularly. Her first pamphlet, *Your Sign is Cuckoo, Girl* (tall-lighthouse) was the Poetry Book Society's Pamphlet Choice for summer 2008. She is currently poet in residence on an allotment for the Apples and Snakes project 'My Place or Yours?'

Cadence

I should consider this cold British soil
an island for a funeral like you do.
But in the cusp between the middle passage
and the *Windrush* something changed
in the chronology of things.

I should imagine someone on a yellow hill,
feeling the same inward discomfort as me
stumbling star-crossed along the planet like me –
but centuries like haunted masts curve between us.
We could trace ourselves to a time
when there were no nations to think of,
when people saw what made them different
and fell in love with it.

Being young is an oxymoron –
our genes are old and as gnarled as the moon.
They are genes only: we're columns of blood biding time,
caught by the delicate cadence that binds us, yes,
but that doesn't mean I owe a thing to you.

Eight

We planted avocado stones all morning until the June
thunder boomed over the garden tamping
the mud with warm rain.

She hurried me in and went back to rescue
The New Yorker and a teal jumper which
lay darkening in the grass.

I drew faces in the misted glass, round-headed, grinning.
When I'd filled the pane with families and houses
I noticed a tap was running –

it was out of time with the steady rain, being water in
a concave bath, but I followed the sound to
the bathroom where the door

pluming with yellow steam stood ajar.
Was that her shadow, long, low, stepping
out of wet clothes?

I watched her ease her apple weight over the side of the bath;
one bristled leg vanished in hot water,
the other stood taut on the mat

and in between something slick, curled, suspended,
that only then, as I glimpsed it from the
wallpapered hall, seemed close

and far from me: familiar and untouchable;
distant, downed; exceptionally there; lithe origami
of moisture and hair.

At last we are alone

At last we are alone
And I can tell you how it felt

To stand in front of a blank wall
And spray 'NF' in white letters

So big they shone against the gloom.

I'm amongst the crowd watching
It being scrubbed from the school wall.

It's eight am. The low clouds are yellow
With rain. Two men in council overalls

Are blasting the thin, erect letters
That salute the dark morning.

My classmates are nervous.
The head teacher, unaware, calls me a thug.

I am a thug. I lie down in the soft grass
After school and rub my bald head.

I call myself *Tom*. I am Tom from 1980:
I am from a story my father told me –

I am Tom who sees my father
And chases him down the street.

[Untitled]

1 *How does she look?*

Jean:
I went in to your room and took
Your diary from the shelf.
I touched the spine with one finger,
Leant it towards me, let it tip
                Leather and heavy
Until it fell in to my hand.
Your room overlooks you Jean.
Your neat room without any possessions
Save a garland of daisies that will be dead
In the morning and this:
             Your cursive hand on cream paper
In ink that appears under a lunar spectrum
Of ash, emulsion, sclera and page.
I sit beside you, reading as you sleep.
You are a bust of talc beneath the linen sheets.

2 *And how will she smell?*

On my last night at the home
          I fed jean food I'd cooked myself.
I wheeled her to the garden
          Where she sat, head rolled to one side,
Staring as I snapped open the Tupperware:
          Kernels of ackee, shards of
White fish; a tangled net of callaloo
          & two glazed slabs of cocoa bread.
There rose the smell of a prior generation –
          The starched steam of the yams,
The fried stickiness of plantains –
          Those smells that once wafted over
Stern tenement blocks and have lingered
          Ever since as a floating inheritance.
The fork bumps her false teeth.
          I wipe away the drool that glistens on her chin.

There are moments when she sits
     Upright and I detect a remote intelligence
Pitted in the dim projectors of her eyes.
     It is so much like staring down a lens
When I gaze at her and push food
     Between her jaws. She opens her mouth
Slowly, deliberately and draws from the fork.
     It is so much a lesson in civility.
Her eager tongue is a momentary signal
     From her roughly-edited mind.

And for desert:
     A banana.

A thick one, still green at the tip,
     One that snaps when I open it –
Full of strands still clinging to the shaft.
     I have half and she has half.
And when we're finished we sit in the
     Cool silence. Jean stirs, as if
She were to speak. She glares hard at beech
     Trees all full of halfling stars.
The banana skin blackens at the crease.
     It softens, browns, begins its slow release
Of humid spores. The lapse, vacant
     Skin and its innocent decay
On the white table, in fading light.
     It is how Jean will look.
It is how she looks already. Slowly
     She is speckling – she is blackening
And reducing in her veined, fragrant skin:
     Already there is an upper note of
Decaying blossom underfoot.
     And below a sparse harmonic:
Spices. Urine. Stagnant. Root.

Yoghurt Pot

My cousin is growing cress in a yoghurt pot.
He is three and perfectly formed. He is free
to sit at the kitchen table with his chin resting
on his hands, waiting for the cress to grow.

The afternoon shadows are moving across him.

I am watching him age. I am watching his eyes
Flicker thousands of times. I am watching him
Bite his nails and then attack the skin around them.
I am watching dozens of plasters stick to and vanish
From his knees. I am watching his spine curve,
And his chin broaden. In his silence, I anticipate
His voice deepen, his sentences thicken, atrophy
And shorten. I wonder about his heart – how fast
It is beating and when it will stop.

I wonder how it feels to have another's heart inside
Me. His heart. A drum like his, hammering its way out.

Come evening he has fallen asleep on the floor.
The earth in the yoghurt pot remains unstirred.
I pick him up and place him in my bedroom,
But I cannot leave as easily as that. We two are alone.
Cars passing below cast their rear-lights on the wall.
I sit beside him, very close, and stare.
Here I am equipped: cavernous me, cooing every month –
A taut, young muscle imagining this boy's slicked head
Slipping through wet, tight elastic –

A wet afternoon shrunk to a red bus
Slurring past a vast estate. Scratched windows.
Tinny hits leaking from an earphone.
      A chicken bone slides back and forth
          In the aisle.
We come to the superstore that draws breath
From everything around it; the one pound shop
      With its leaning towers of garish tack.
I honestly don't know which I prefer:
      The bored employee or the pot bellied shop owner;
      The girl with orbits dangling from her ears or the girl
      With the peculiar god, bangled and painted in a
      Procession of relatives –
And I don't know if I can talk:
      My eyes are English spectacles and everywhere
I see decay; I see cheap shoes; I see fast food; I see women
With fake hair and plastic gems on their toenails.
I see pierced children. I see bags in the trees and animal entrails
On the road. I see damp take-away boxes. I smell weed.
I hear a girl call her son a dickhead when he cries.
      And who am I to judge?
      And if I don't, who will?
      And who knows the depth of my hypocrisy
When I cross the road,
When I change seat,
When I move to another carriage,
      To avoid the sound and the smell?
    One night a boy comes upstairs
And begins playing music from his phone.
      I ask him to stop and he ignores me.
      I ask him again and he stares.
When we are alone, I take a sword from my bag
And cut upwards from the navel to the chops.
I draw him and set alight each quarter.

EMILY BERRY

Emily Berry was born in London in 1981. She has an MA in Creative and Life Writing from Goldsmiths' College and an MA in English Literature from Leeds University. Her poems have been published in various magazines including *The Manhattan Review*, *Poetry London* and *Stop/Sharpening/Your/Knives*. In 2007 she won commendations in the Bridport Prize and the Poetry London competition, and in 2008 she received an Eric Gregory Award from the Society of Authors. Her pamphlet, *Stingray Fevers*, was published by tall-lighthouse in 2008. Emily also works as a freelance copyeditor of novels and non-fiction, while alter-ego Poppy Tartt reviews breakfasts at www.londonreviewofbreakfasts.co.uk.

The Incredible History of Patient M.

I went swimming with the Doctor;
he wore his stethoscope and listened
to the ebb and flow. *Bad line*, he said.

I hid the stones in my pockets.
I'm in training with the Doctor –
I'm closely monitored.

He straps his velcro cuff to my bicep
and pumps it till I'm breathless.
You need to breathe more, he says.

On Thursdays he examines me
on all fours. He wears a white coat
with too-short sleeves.

He can't work out why I'm so heavy.
His wrists are great hairy chunks,
and he wears no watch.

Time is nothing, says the Doctor.
He's unconventional. *Time is nowhere,*
like a dead bird in a cave. Let's take a look inside.

I'd never opened up before. The Doctor
has a scalpel. *And I'm not afraid to use it!*
He calls it his shark's tooth.

The Doctor bites and leaves a mark
like the fossil of a sprung jaw.
He slapped my face with his penis.

To get you going, he said. My heart is now
on red alert, apparently. *If it stops,*
he reminds me, you're dead.

I ♥ NY

No one told me Times Square was a triangle.
Last time we came your uncle showed us round
and I felt proud of Piccadilly Circus.
This time we came by train from Canada –
the half-unfrozen Hudson was cracking up
so gorgeously, and the clouds seemed to send down
light like spaceships marking where to land.
At the border a bearded man was taken away.

In New York their faces light up when you speak.
We bought socks in the gift shop of some big hotel
off Broadway; it was free art Friday and there was
suddenly a blizzard and we'd been soaked to the knee.

I love you both, but it did my head in queuing
for that Japanese restaurant. Katie and I
did Edward Scissorhands with chopstick wrappers.
When the food arrived it looked like it was moving
and I absolutely freaked. You have to say
wadder, or they won't get it.

That was the day after I walked past Barnes & Noble
and the *Collected Poems* of Dylan Thomas
fell from the sky. No, really! And they say a penny
dropped from the Empire State could kill a man,
so a book could really do some damage.
You can buy non-sequiturs in bundles now
from international supermarkets. And guilt,
where is that sold? How much for eating cupcakes
on my birthday from the famous bakery
and admiring San Franciscan boys in Aviators? Oh –
and when we went for mani-pedis, we sat in a row
and Korean ladies kneeled at our feet.

What I Did On My Summer Holidays

Did you know I bought you a present
when they minded me that summer in Wales,
the summer you tried to get better taking anti-depressants
in a hospital in Archway on a hill, and your hands
shook when you had visitors, and they told me
you loved me very much? The last time I saw you
was in a McDonald's. I don't remember what I ate.
My cousin tells me we bought stick-on earrings
from a stall on Oxford Street and stuck them on.
The last time I spoke to you was on the phone.
I don't remember what I said. Your present I kept
for myself, a pink candle in the shape of an owl,
because when I got home there was no one
to give it to.
            She was only a child when you sent her
across flooded deserts, on horseback. Through
never-ending rain she rode as if she knew how,

her sopping feet inside her ribboned socks,
the hard dark reins in her frozen hands, the poor horse
wading cloaked in black like he was dressed
for mourning too. You'd done your deed by then.
There were trees: they were sodden, many-
branched, clawing her glazed cheeks like witches.
The sky fell and fell. Through all this she travelled
to land on islands where they took her into a grip
and pinched so. She was alone and had no coat on.

Structure (or lack of) is vital in this poem

Questions I Wanted to Ask You in the Swimming Pool

Didn't you see me standing in the shallow end, looking out at you from
blue goggles with alien eyes? Didn't you swim over, in this other life,
wiping water from your cheeks, to say *I'm getting out now, don't be long*?
Didn't I take too long in the shower as usual and meet you, by your bike,
finishing off a packet of Wheat Crunchies, and didn't you say you couldn't
        believe
that I hadn't left you any as usual? Didn't my wet hair leak two damp patches
down the front of my top, till I looked like a mother with no one to feed?
Didn't you promise, whatever happened, you would always find me attractive?
When we got home didn't I dry my hair for ages on the loudest setting
while you cooked and shouted comments I couldn't hear, and didn't we laugh,
worn out enough to relax with each other for once, for the moment forgetting
that everything was actually fucked; how many times did we drift together,
        tired,
regret tautening over the bones of us the way skin does as it dries?

My Perpendicular Daughter

My perpendicular daughter grew taller
than they said she would do when I got her;
I wish they hadn't lied to me like that.

29

I thought a daughter would be light and quiet –
not at all; they hung her upside down inside me
and now she sticks straight out, gets in the way

when I stand close to walls. I tried to take her back
but they said I should be glad a man had known me
and I'd only got what I'd been begging for.

Would I like a booklet? Instead I asked for milk
and tipped its long white screech right down,
it furred my throat and stayed there, curdling

all afternoon. There are no returns on daughters,
they pointed out. I aimed her at them like a gun:
This is how death begins, I told them.

A Short Guide to Corseting

My first was an eighteen-inch black ribbon,
straight off the rack; my boyfriend picked it out.
We agreed small waists were more attractive;
we were in a loving and supportive relationship.

Choosing her trainer is a tightlacer's last and
most important act. Look for a man with faith
and hands strong enough to teach you how to
give yourself away. Don't be afraid of restraint.

Pain is the spine of life. It holds you up.
I wear a corset for these reasons: love came
sideways, like a crab. I wanted to agree with
love; I wanted to be carried off in its claws.

My trainer keeps me corseted twenty-three
hours a day. Any less is a waste of time. I love
his arms, thick as pythons. Every morning he
tightens the laces till they burn lines in his palms,

till he swears under his breath and apologises.
I cling to the doorframe. This is harder for him
than for me. I've seen how he fights to contain
himself. This hurts us both. That's a good thing.

My second was a sixteen-inch with a two-inch stem.
I had it made to measure. My boyfriend held me
firm while the corsetier laced me in. I drew my
last deep breaths and I gave myself up then,

standing between them. It was such a relief. *Yes*,
the corsetier said. *Perfect fit*. My breasts frothed
like champagne from a bottle. My eyes bulged.
Little skittle, my trainer whispered. I couldn't bend.

A wrinkle ran down my back like a seam. Now
that I wear a fourteen-inch I use only the top half of
my lungs; there's just room to breathe. I've still got
more than enough. I've realised how little we need.

The Mother's Tale

Don't come crying to me with your fables, the mother declared
the day her daughter went into the world. I won't share a drop
of emotion. I forced myself through the eye of a needle
to give you breath and now you're stepping out with no word to me
as if you were spun from a prayer. Oh wipe that face off, she sighed.
There's not an ocean I haven't dreamed of and never set sail on.
There's not a wind could twist the hair from my neck and whirl me
off my feet like a giddy belle. There's not a sky hasn't fallen
like a shroud. My girl, at the end of the day I couldn't care less
for my bones. I was tacking the bleeding seams of your heart before
you even knew how to love. Observe how thin I've become.
I wore myself to this raggedy thread so I could run your life
right through. From jaw to wicked neck dear, down to the arches
of your feet, you'll feel my stitches flinch inside you as you run.

AMY BLAKEMORE

Amy Blakemore was born in 1991, and began writing poetry when she was 15. She was named a Foyle Young Poet of the Year in both 2007 and 2008, and was commended in the Torbay Open Poetry Competition in 2008. That same summer she interned at the Poetry Society, and they taught her to photocopy and do other useful things. Her poetry has been published in a variety of magazines and journals, including *Pomegranate*, *Cadaverine*, *Iota* and *Rising*. She has also read her work on BBC London 94.9 and Radio Europe. She currently divides her time between trampolines in East Dulwich and swings in Deptford.

Crab in a Polystyrene Crate

You are spiking rocks green-fed
in flaking ice-bed so far from
your tepid rock-pool mouth
with its tender fringe of algae.

Crab in a polystyrene crate,
your eyes are still so impossibly small,
but does your sidecoded disc-brain, ridged,
remember minnow-crushing Sundays,

your sisters' hands like stinging orchids
as they were lifted in the swash?

Discos on a dead sailor's femur,
humpbacked quicksteps.

Dead crab in a polystyrene crate,
for sale on a market stall –
do the eels beside you sometimes writhe
through their rubber death damp?

Ask you why you didn't try harder
to snap the ropes,
un-net the nets?

The Virgin of Guadalupe

From the playground to the park,
she tore indiscriminately,

her hair wide behind her like a
flag; dripping with catholica,

purple and gold rosaries
at her snaky body's every juncture;

velvet ribbon and scraps of lurex,
blue Marys and Theresas.

Through the city she blazed a trail,
her mouth became a firetrap;

she smelt of men
with motorbikes and vintage ephemera.

They called her The Virgin of Guadalupe,
for all her nailgunned roses, her weeping messiahs;

though the name was ironic.
You heard she mothered

noisily behind
the bus shelter at dusk.

In the summer her hair would burn
and the shrines she kept behind her ears would melt,

she'd tear through the city in ankle socks
and not much else.

It won't be long you see,
before she tears no more –

becomes a legend
for the sewer's glitterati

and perhaps
cleans rooms in a hotel somewhere.

The Guests

You are a child, imagine it.
You stop at doorways to squint at guests
sleeping like alligators on sofas and sofabeds.

They are your parents' lovers or friends.

You watch them because they lie between you and the television.

You stop because the creases of their eyes
are crusted yellow like salt caves,
seem a little old, a little wise,

and because you feel their snoring breaths,
hacked from the sour morning air
form tacky resin statuettes when you aren't there

of pearly-beaked doves or women in ball gowns

that will tell you who these strangers are.

Achievement

On this last day there is a kind of noisy peace
as cans of Carling and Silly String
are passed through the dimlit laughter and ignition remix.

Girls come sheathed in chiffon and satin,
bee-sting tits, filmy lips,
waistlength gold chains that they finger nervously.

Gowns rustle like small birds
in the thumping undergrowth,
damp brushings through the bass,
they bounce and grind

and balloons like swollen growths inhabit the orange shadow,
the guy from IT is DJing –
J20 at the bar.

Some hang in the twilight outside
wrapped in their boyfriends' suitjackets
watching the sunset cherry the sky.

They kick the heels off their scarlet-stripped feet.

This is a precursor to our future Christmas office parties,
but here the boobs are perter, boys are prettier,
cellulite is the wolf from magazine adverts.

No alcohol provided and the soberness is killing me,
I haven't gone far when you grab me, drag me to the floor.

Yes, I dance.
Yes, you are a God.

Fallen silver streamers glitter in corners like smashed braces,

and the only thing I have achieved in school is you.

Making Money

He wore suits as thick as calluses and had
a certain bird-poise. Waspy stillness.

He knew that night in London
was not black or even Egyptian blue
but red, with a texture like leopard print, bad coffee.

Once he cut loose and shouted
a demon call to prayer
to the cement quadruplexes, iron heiresses,

the perplexing republic of drunken city traders;
but you don't make money when you cut loose.

And this guy,
he made money.

Played his way on the pulsing magnificence
of the city,

the unrest
in the trees.

The Stalklands

In the old Stalklands
we dealt stumpside in milkteeth
and marbles.

Remember the birds that frappered
green-beaked in the low bushes?

That day we split the heavy slab
that hid the ant's nest and saw
ant-eggs. The colour of pinch,
they were silked with small white hairs.

And the bedroom window that opened itself to the heat,
the burning tarmac, 90s hits on translucent
plastic tapes, the three blonde
daughters and the porcelain dolls, empty-eyed.

Returning to the old Stalklands,
the leaves are dusty,
flowers have no pungency.

A boy in a football shirt darts from the undergrowth.

Sweet, Seedless

I got a satsuma naked.

I peeled back its wax,
thumb waded in to the cuticle,
a shock of blonde rind on each side.

I found it babyheading in my palm
or an old man's head underfinger,
soft wet skull,

(cannot withstand the effects
of careless handling)

bang of blonde rind on each side,
the hard white string bits

biting-almost-lilac
tiny guts.

And each capillaried side
fish-like.

SIDDHARTHA BOSE

Siddhartha Bose was born in Calcutta in 1979. His early years were split between Bombay and Calcutta. A seven-year itch in the USA followed. He trained as an actor and made short films. His work has appeared in journals including *The Wolf*, *Fulcrum*, *Tears in the Fence*, *Eclectica* and *Alhamra Literary Review*. He lives in London, where he's performed his work at literary events such as La Langoustine est Morte, Plum and New Blood, and playing venues including the Whitechapel Gallery, the Troubadour and the Royal College of Art. He's recently featured as a poet on Resonance FM, the City of London Festival, the Battle of Ideas Festival and the London Word Festival. Sid co-hosts *Beeswax*, a new live poetry night in the East End. He also teaches poetry and Shakespeare, while writing a PhD on the grotesque at Queen Mary, University of London.

Nameless

I

I was always an accomplice actor.

In my onewindowed room
I heard voices at weddings in
Cities where mothers know the
Glint of the moon, the spark of the cold.

These chants soar high to the
Cracks in my ceiling; become the ravens of
Beethoven's last quartets; choruses to a goddess
By the Ganges, her skin as silt, black – her
Tongue limp, red with shame.

A fine wedding this –
Fugues of blood.

II

Shhh...

Red wine, a mosquito bite on my hand.

The rattle of rifles – sporadic
Rain that summer – outside our
Home in Calcutta –
A communist city,
No place for faith.

A mosque was raped in the north.

The city shuts. My mother eats the curls of her hair.
Hear the guns, shona! Hear the guns!
A child of twelve.
In my father's absence, I invoke:

A street named after an Urdu poet where I was
Greeted with a smile by a leper
Balding with disease, her arms
Hanging like carcasses, her teeth
Black, her eyes – sweating streets
Of the city – crowded, with flies.

She held a dog's mouth in her fist.
Not alive, not dead.

The city forms in veins.
Cut open.

III

I saw her for the next five months.
She watched me, sniffing – a
Huntsman on all fours – rain,
Sweat, typhoid, falling from my
Skin in bombs.

IV

Hungry. Need medicine. Crack
My knuckles. Gets
Cold at night. Mosquitoes. Pirates. Planes.
Flies on muttonsticks.
Partition. Brothers shaved my head. Others tied
Me by the legs. Whipped me. My nostrils groaned.
The smell of coalmines.

Poisha dao!

The whiff of sandstone –
In Rajasthan, had mirrors on my dress.
A woman, pale skin, straddled the seas, gave it me.
Draped on head by wave of silk,
Red and yellow long snake on my lap...

V

I wade past the nightgirls,
Darkred bangles clattering,
Men with needles in arms seated round a temple like lotuses,
A rickshawpuller who starts selling hash, changes his name,
Becomes a Hindu just before the fast,

Couples stepping out of Japanese cars,
To make it on time for
Rehearsals of Chekhov's short stories and plays.

VI

Shhh...

I write to her, my modernmedusa.
Smug. (A can of soup, in America).

Not alive, not dead.

Animal City

I

Twin-bride of my ten-head home, I
    Watch you closely from the
    Cross of scorched lands, rubble of sea-foam,
        Fire of snake-tongue.

Grand and pungent in act, I long to write you an epic,
Worthy of our ancient tales.

For now, these
    Bites will do, as I
    Chrome myself round your lingo,
Scalding my brow with your
Tears of grime, shame, bigtalk wealth.

I gender you in full-on
    Curry angrezi, with
Patois political, image transcontinental.

II

Close on nine years you
    Be my multiverse, *Bombay meri jaan.*

Now me your bastard
    Ratshipper, who you coldthaw by turns,
    Breaking limbs, tossing one by one after
        Chop-'n'-changing me to your

Dogs that bark the
    Rounds of Kala Ghoda.

III

Me you fat in slums stomach-lining
    Chatrapati Shivaji International airport,

Me you snatch like the sea necklace by
Marine Drive,

Me you step underfoot towards the
    Mosque that grows from the sea, by
Hajiali, breaking me into the south.

Me you bleed on treetops that crown Siddhi-Vinayak,
    Pole-vaulting through cricket parks, churchbells,
Lion in Sion.

Me you gorge in dark Bandra sounds,
    With India electronica, the asli bhangra.

Me you lick in clamour bars of Juhu,
    Palm trees and pork by the sea-view.

Me you sweat in pav bhaji streets, pani-puri
    Gag, vada pao itch.

Me you wet in tobacco nights, incense from
    Nigerian peddlars in Colaba, fevered.

    IV

You are my crude health, the
    Crass in my conscience.

(Once, one of your statue saints called out, at the
    Curve of Mahim, as the smog of sun
    Cut through canopy trees in
Cockroach antennae:

'Life's an echo. You get back what you give.')

I remember too much. I insurrect. I thaw.

    V

Recalling me pullin out ear-wax,
    Galling me, heavy and brown and long like rat shit, by
    Cuffe Parade at the ballpoint pen-tip of South Bombay.
        I see through large French windows, fishing-nets, seasalt.
        Wood smells like horsehide.

On the bus back to Versova, home from school, my
     Math teacher yells me 'bout
     Them Goan sausages, how spicy they be, how
          Mother would like them.

My first love, Aditi, in the school closeby
     Amitabh Bachchan's house. I thought her an
     Androgyne, as in my child-wet dreams, we'd
          Fly over electric grass, whitelight in Andheri.

But no no, I tell it straight, one
     Image stark stays, genuine.

VI

We stop on Linking Road in days when Fiats
     Clogged the shape of traffic towards Mahim Causeway, north
                                             to south.

Long before the whip of olive bars, mojo melts, too school for cool
                                             drawl-mocking
Mumbaikars, sultry and bangled Bandra girls, their
          Slurps inviting.

Back in the 80s, a few years before I
     Played football with a bat-blind cancered grandfather, my
     Mother 'n' me stop at the corner where Waterfield Road spills.

(Nearby, Maa liked the cottage-cheese shop.)

As we wait for the green light, a
     Sadhu six-footed walks to my openaired window,
     Dreads-matted, beard in forest, saffron-covered with
          Hint of charcoal, fume, lavender.

Him have a sleek, spotted,
     Jazz-patterned python wrapped round his
     Upper torso, fitted perfect like a bride's sari. The snakehead
                                             juts out
     In a slither above his locks.

43

He stretches them crow hands, pigeon nails,
    Towards me, eyes fired, jaundiced yellow.

I recoil, screaming. A
    Hijra on the street-divider claps his hands,
    Clacks like a witch. Light greens, cars cough, cop
        Blinks. Maa shakes.

VII

Them surrealists were hacks, term-tablers, scabs on a
    Tired, Southern Europe.

They never knew you, O animal city, where a thousand gods
    Jostle like men hanging outta late-evening suburban trains,
    Rowdy, brutal, bleeding.

Now some call you Mayanagri, but in me –
    Traitor – you be the slick oil, the
    Steel breath, the becoming cancerous starshape of a
        Fresh from sleep, proud,
Seething century.

Author's note: 'Mayanagri' translates, popularly, as 'city of dreams'.
A 'hijra' is a eunuch.

Chinatown, New York

A nose for paradox
Made me read Chuang-Tzu
On a late autumn afternoon
In Washington Square –

From his butterfly dream
I too emerged with wings,
A flowing gown of red and green,
A taste for wet fingertips.

I wafted down Mott Street –
Bees in my hair,
Pollen on my tongue,
Rain coiling in my eyes.

From your curious castle, heavy,
In a bowl hammered out of lapis lazuli,
You gave me thick soup
Cooked in the entrails of a fatted fish.

In it, strands of the Milky Way
Welcoming, cradling me
From the sluggish approach of
Snow, heating bills, a fading lover.

Mother's Lament

The Pietà is renewed –

She sits on a road skulled with tanks,
While green hills round this burnt bulletholed town
Gape at her breasts, ripe as Arabian mangoes.
They hover over the lips of a young, frostbitten man.

His head is a clock.
His right arm, a bow.
His beard, shy.

She wonders
Running her fingers, draped in blood,
On a parching forehead.

She wheels through the sky,
Leaking bones:

'Oh, the shiver o' my spine,
The salt o' my eyes,
The beam o' the sun,
The love o' my life –

Drink of this pure, fresh milk
And remember to say your prayers.
I cooked you biriyani today
And your aunt has sent you sweets.
I washed your clothes so you'd look a butterfly.
I saw the girl outside the chai shop,
The one who charmed your father na!
Remember?
Your friends wait to
Play their awful games,
And your letters are in order.

(The general gorges nails, cuts in mud
Struts through city-gates,
Lotus in eye.
He plucked my tooth, betel-stained, for a souvenir.)

Tomorrow you must wash your hair,
You must read your books.

Tomorrow, I'll put you to sleep, my chand ka tukra.
I'll tell you many silly stories.

Remember to share your secrets
And I will show you, the world is
Truly beautiful.'

AILBHE DARCY

Ailbhe Darcy was born in 1981 and grew up on the south side of Dublin, near Dundrum. She has a degree in English and French at University College Dublin, which included a year in France, at the University of Nanterre. While at UCD she was deeply involved with the university's English Literary Society, through which she met Clodagh Moynan; and the two now co-edit *Moloch*. After receiving her BA, Ailbhe completed an MA in Publishing at University of the Arts, London, before returning to Dublin to do an MSc in Development Studies. She's is now studying for a PhD in contemporary poetry at the University of Notre Dame, in Indiana. A first pamphlet of her poems with tall-lighthouse in 2009 will be followed by a first book-length collection from Bloodaxe in 2010.

He tells me I have a peculiar relationship with my city

As though I were something divorced
from the skin I'm in, could scrap or elope
with my own tattooed scapula, pouting belly, saddle curve
of his palm's kiss.

But here's the vein on my left wrist
fat as Liffey, my right skinny
lost Dodder; slit,
they run murky and thick
with city. My left breast
thingmote, my right sugarloaf,
my throat a high and narrow pane, frogged
and pointed like a lancet.

My country stretches from a ham's span
outside the pale to the top
of Parnell street. I cannot leave.
It is a narrow, self-effacing swathe,
the shape of me –
enough scar to fret at, too close to desire or despise.
If Dublin is kicks in the shins,
my shin is its sweet spot, summer lunchtime Stephen's Green.

Panopticon

*Only don't, I beseech you, generalise too much in these sympathies
and tendernesses – remember that every life is a special problem
which is not yours but another's, and content yourself with the terri-
ble algebra of your own.*
    HENRY JAMES, in a letter to a friend

We are up to our pits in Sunday papers
when my father says that things never used to happen
when he was growing up. He means
the black crawly crawly Darfur fly, man
on a leash, girl with burns, crumpled machinery
at Inishowen, and he means Matthew,

who died last night at last of madness.
My father and I at the eye of the panopticon,
two of Prometheus' descendants, bound
at the centre of a shrinking globe. Sometimes
he used to turn the television off, newspapers
would grow angular holes
where bloodshed had been. Now it's I
who want to fold cranes of the papers for him,
build bonfires of TV sets.
It circles us, the noise, all the same. When people ran
from the falling towers, they stopped
to buy cameras, stood
with their backs to the towers to watch
the house of cards fall
over and over on shop window screens. No wonder
perhaps that you with your too much of gentleness
wanted out, and we did not stop you.
Your friends expect to weigh forever
what we could have given
against what we could not change.
What kind of algebra would it take?
Matthew, love, I carry myself with care on Mondays.
I lie to hairdressers. I walk. I carry a notebook
to write down feelings
in case I need them again. I pretend
to be someone else at traffic lights. I stay clear
of mirrors, newspapers sometimes. I live
as best I can. I do the awful maths.

Caw Poem

Not atriums and ventricles that cup and pour
but a solitary magpie
beats cricked wings
against my ribcage walls:

oil-slippery, bug-ugly,
reflecting every colour and none,
playing I-Spy with the gleams of a mind,

singing hoarse and low:

you I caw to be a map   a metronome   a distance left to run
a red wheelbarrow beside white chickens   the lion for real
a rose by any other name   a word that has been won
a tangerine and spit the pips   days beyond the rhododendrons
a Huffy Henry hid the day
a madeleine   a dare to eat a peach   a pomegranate   a persimmon
a long cold drink of water   you
                    Chimborazo
                        Xanadu

                        Calloo
                            Callay

                    Weialala leia la   lei

Edith said of the poet
that he was quite cracked
but that was where the light squeaked through.
I must have taken it as a clue.

I cocked my head
hopped a little, hopped a little closer,
love become a scrum, a scuffle,
a ruffle of feathers

as though I could
rifle through you,
plunder some bright thing,
learn to sing true.

The Llamas for Real

There are crocuses and daffodils all over Cambridge
and I do not know what to do with their promise.
I have no kind in this fen,
in these claret-swilled ditches, no kith nor ken.
Calcified taps, faces brush-mouthed like whales,

the Cam cold with rowers, the walls damp with snails,
I rifle through the dictionary I rented with my room:
foxed; dog-eared; out of date; blue.

Willing epiphany, I at least saw some llamas –
three in a Cambridgeshire field, ready to spring. They murmured,
'*There is no there there.* No Father Christmas,
no Plath and Hughes, no dahut or grue.
You can take your picture all round the world like a gnome,
but you'll never sneeze hard enough to be freed of your soul.'

I wished I'd not come. In Bristol, at least,
there was a gadget that had pointed the way
to the Earth's core; tenth planet, Neptune; the moon.

The Room

> *his suffocated voice resumes*
> *its dreary innuendo:*
> *there are other ways to leave the room*
> *than the door and the window.*
>
> DON PATERSON, 'Bedfellows'

I

There are more ways to leave the room
than the door and the great bay-window,
but the exit may not take you.

The warren of links riddling your screen
with routes may all burrow back to your own catacomb.
The newspaper that unfolds like a trick,

predicting fortunes, might, laid out to be waked,
prove a map of tricks you've missed,
things you were too frightened to do

or to stop and you just kept walking –
round, in a loop. And the velveteen dreams
you think you can lean back into,

taking the weight off, putting down time,
catnap you, frogmarch you, pigdog you
back to the zoo turned kangaroo court

where you are tried, found human,
found wanting, found making a dash
for the door, and sentenced back into the room.

II

'There are no more ways to leave the room
than the window. No more shall I push
the door, that hard labour
that quickmarches me along the path of least resistance,
the road most taken, the exit into the mindless
masses of spectators. The wallpaper

along the stairs down to the street is yellow
and monstrous, the street sweats damp,
and in the hallway I have seen a rat turn
and answer my prayers with globe-eyed scorn
before waddling back into the shadows.
The shadows seething in corners only bide

their time, and every time I brave
that long walk down to the street
I am taking my life into my hands.

So I am taking an executive decision. Set it down
that I left the room in the only way left to such a man:
by the window, arms outstretched, going forward.'

Legacy

and finally, a screed for my children.
To you I leave the all-you-can-eat buffet,
the tall and grande coffee cups,
the sword swallower, the champion pork pie eater,
the television's unstinting hunger,

our own slow immigration,
and the night your mother wept silently,
not understanding I was too exhausted for desire.
Ñamma ñamma, my son, my daughter,
you have eaten all my love –
all you can eat.

Reject the world as parataxis,
the quick syllepsis,
the fall into the egotistical sublime.
If the able stay indoors,
thugs will take over the agora.
So sing the descant chord,
sing it in a field, to open sky,
to you I leave it to win
each word over again, one word at a time –
gnamma gnamma.

To you I leave each full night's sleep.
At night, too tired to rest,
I have stroked your backs for wings.
There is a there there.
When a death happens
in the family, booking the flight
will feel like doing something,
a Nyemi Nyemi.
Forgive your father
his age, his accent.
I leave you your perspective –

look back sometimes.
When you were smaller, more pliant,
we took you to see sights.
Once a tour guide declared,
'if you have a camera, you can take pictures.
If you don't, you can't. Simple as that.'
Numen. Numen. We had to hush you,
concerned you'd disturb the other visitors,
for you saw no reason not to laugh and laugh.
I leave you that simple as.

JOE DUNTHORNE

Joe Dunthorne was born in 1982 in Swansea, where he grew up. His debut novel, *Submarine*, won the Curtis Brown Prize and was shortlisted for the Bollinger Wodehouse Prize for comic fiction. It's been translated in to six languages. His poetry has been published in various magazines, including *Poetry Review*, *New Welsh Review* and *Magma*, and he has written for the *Independent* and *Guardian*. His work has been read on Channel 4, Radio 3 and Radio 4. His Faber New Poets pamphlet is forthcoming in 2010. He is a striker for the England Writers' Football Team. There is no Welsh Writers' Team. He lives in London.

Cave dive

> *Every sixteen metres of depth is equivalent to one alcoholic drink.*
> MAURO BERTOLINI, The Diver's Handbook

He looks up through panels of light:
pre-orthodontic limestone, groupers
sulking in threes, the sky peering in
from blue-green slots like the lamp fittings
of his youth.
        He remembers being six,
lying on his back beneath a kitchen chair,
gazing up at his father's unmapped nostrils,
his mother's skirt riffling past like a spotted
eagle ray. Underneath the dining table,
he found pencil marks: a quarter-circle
and two words underscored. *Possible Extension.*
At six, it was a code or, perhaps,
the solution to a code.

At sixty-five metres,
it takes a blue whale's long blink to recall
what one plus one turns in to. His slow mind
thinks time is just another surface, he can pass
through the swirling halocline that keeps us
from our pasts:
                    the fresh and the preserved.
He's back in his father's study, pouring
a bag of marbles across the rug. In the glow
from the tentacled lampshade, he holds
up his Bosser, sees himself swimming
in its spiral reef.
                    Taking out his respirator,
he is either young or drunk. From his lips
he scatters balls of glass.

Filters

My big sister rings to say she is riding around
on the back of Richard's motorbike
and would I like to meet for a drink.
Richard is a married man.
My sister is gay and I am always
dropping this in to conversation.

She has a helmet under her arm
and a rum with ginger beer.
I sometimes ask my sister
if she has dismantled the patriarchal hegemony yet,
which is a joke. Her ex-girlfriend used to say
that every bar should have a non-male space,
just like you have non-smoking.

We're talking about marathon training.
The pub is beneath a brick railway bridge. The light
is greenish and you can feel the invisible trains.
Out front, they're selling oysters on a school desk.
My sister says, How about it?
When we were young, we used to fight.

She chipped my tooth with a doorstop.
I will eat anything.

The oysters smell of tin foil.
They are still alive.

My sister thinks I should chew a few times;
Richard says I should swallow it whole.
The creature is in my mouth
and now I must decide.

The Gambler

He lets women spin through his mind.
Blurred at first, the reel slows – a lemon,
a seven, a cherry, then stops at Maria
from the library. Spilling her art books
– Rubens, Vermeer – she lands on the mattress.
Her body emits an oven-fresh glow.

On the bed next to her a mannequin
becomes Britt Ekland's body double,
becomes his ex in a duffel bag
before halting at the girl from the lido –
the one with the body he can't imagine dry.
Wearing just a two-piece and her certificates,

she arrives. Finally, he flicks through
some of his male friends, those he thinks
more capable, more probable, before boldly
picking himself, with one decisive nudge,
he emrges in the doorway, naked,
nothing if not perpendicular. Lazily,

he allows the bedroom to be the bedroom
he is actually in: sponge-print wall paint
and stacks of old cassettes, organised
by mood. He edits out *The Queen is Dead*
and, in her sway, has Prince's *Greatest Hits*.
He redecorates his mind to match:

silk sheets appear like the tablecloth trick,
reversed; in lieu of a lens to Vaseline,
a low lying mist descends. And in the scene
that follows, there's no logistics, no awkward
shifts of weight, just a series of flash cuts:
from one geometric shape to the next

– apple, anvil, bell – no stopping
for the runner to re-douse Girl Two
with chlorinated water. Maria adapts
classical poses: she's Leda, he's the Swan;
they role-play the rape of Leucippus's
daughters; pearl earrings scatter;

Banana, horseshoe, pear. They're on
the cash board, turrets strobing.
He starts to open and close his eyes,
the shuttered Hi/Lo between this world
and that, then the churn of his coinage
at last paying out. The cash on his chest.

The girls he left behind. He would
feed it back in, if he could.

A disastrous campaign in bohemia

In a gutted outside broadcast van
we took off for the Altamont Speedway,
throwing ash trays to the wind
– *set 'em free, Maria, set 'em free* –
and rode unwelcomed in to Livermore,
took off our shirts, played hacky sack
on their fundamental lawns,
got sunburnt and called it napalm,
said we were sisters and brothers.

I made love to Maria in the Berkeley
fountain, let our bodies send
a message, let our mouths tend our bodies.

When the summer was over
and Charlie Manson's arrest reminded
us to call our families, the hopes
we'd hosted began to fade.
The college friends we heard were dead
seemed even cooler now.

Worship

When picking your spot, look for a balance
of elements. Always show respect to those
wearing lower factors than you. Always check
downwind before shaking out your towel.

Lie back. Let the sand make a duplicate
of your spine. Match your breath to the tide.
Clear away all thoughts (now that wasn't
so tough). Let your body do the thinking.

On the backs of your eyelids, you will likely
see your childhood sweetheart in flames,
flailing around, doused in lamp oil. This is natural.
Let her dance. You deepen by the hour.

Future Dating

Sat along rotating laminate benches,
we wear scrolling badges that display:
Name; Favourite thing; Emotional state.
I am Joe; Money; Anxious
as Porcia; Old buildings; Extraordinary
swivels into view with art deco
cheekbones, sky-rise posture.

She speaks in intricate structures
with witty stucco asides
and is either marriage material
or a one-off demolition-fuck
in a room full of Lego.
I give her green as she dioramas
into Karen; Knitting; Distracted:
her chopsticks clicking
as though making a scarf
from her udon noodles;
our three minutes pass in excruciating
knit one purl one chit-chat.
She sucks up her tongue
and draws a frowning emoticon
in the air, before swishing away
as George; The Nineties; Superior
slides over, saying she likes my retro avatar
and it turns out we both still use Mozilla
'Keepin' it old skool!'
– High five –
'LOL!'
then our three minutes are gone
and I'm thumping green
as Sylvia; Firearms; Impatient
appears: shotgun eyes, fingers twitching,
white gunk at the corners of her mouth.
I smell her feet from under the table:
fragrance of murderer's glove
and I'm pressing red and red
as Kate; Imperfections; Unclear
pulls up with semi-translucent hair.
I compliment her body, her lips,
the infinite detail of her eyes
but she says she can take no credit.
Then she's screaming, quietly,
that her battery's about to die
as she starts to fizz like an unearthed plug.

MIRIAM GAMBLE

Miriam Gamble was born in Brussels in 1980 and grew up in Belfast. She studied at Oxford and at Queen's University Belfast, where she recently completed a PhD in contemporary British and Irish poetry. She won an Eric Gregory Award in 2007. Her poems have appeared in *The Rialto, The Yellow Nib, Succour, Gallous, Fortnight* and the *Ulster Tatler*. Her pamphlet, *This Man's Town*, was published by tall-lighthouse in 2007, and her first book-length collection, *The Squirrels Are Dead*, is due from Bloodaxe in 2010. She has worked as a pony-trekking guide, a waitress and a university tutor; she currently works part-time for an independent bookshop, and is on the lookout for a proper job.

The Flaying of Marsyas

It's said the Muses judged the contest –
that they were pleased by Apollo's superior craft.
His ability to lift the pelt in a single stroke
was greatly lauded. 'See how beautiful the work,
clean as the average man would skin an orange!'
they remarked among themselves. 'Not even a wound
disturbs his fearful symmetry.' Meanwhile Marsyas

lay on, his life force startlingly undiminished,
limbs gesturing in disbelieving contract
with the world. 'This for a stupid pipe,' he roared,
for Marsyas, Ovid relates, possessed the gift
of consciousness: 'for this they cleave me from myself!'
But nobody beyond the forest heard his cries,
and Marsyas's body, reverting now to the status

of a brute, dumb animal, went on in hopeful
disbelieving, heart thumping away in the blue furnace
of itself, lungs fighting leafy crusts (an organ,
so anatomists tell us, so wonderfully porous
it survives in the transfer from a body to another body),
tears stinging his flittered cheeks, for a full
half turning of the sundial before darkness came

upon him, and he curled into position like a dog.

Ichi-no-tani

The emperor's goods are sinking through the water.
Rich pickings – the quality of the regal larder
is such even the toothiest of the water monsters
does not let its yellow eye from the ball for long enough
to be drawn to the muddle of flailing limbs – there,
and there, again! – seeking to interrupt the meal
with death's slow fanfare. Death, as ever,

comes roving out in search of witnesses:
the emperor is willing to sacrifice a toe, even
an elbow, so long as there be more to it than this:
more to the felling of an empire than the sharp cries
of his wailing mother, face splattered with kohl,
her hair a mess; than the ricocheting passage
of a skiff over tranquil waters. In the shallows,

rough women loot his mother's vanity case,
left bobbing by the shore in her distress,
and the sea creatures murmur in the moon-pale flicker,

watching the slow descent of gorgeousness –
item, a jewel-crusted dagger; item, a ceremonial dress –
spiralling through the ever darkening layers.
The prince Yoshitsune is dead; also dead,

his mother, who sculled on the sea's cold mirror
till she could scull no more. When, later,
Bashō comes here, he will write of the prince's death
in cumbersome prose, his eye drawn rather
to the impregnability of the water's surface,
the octopuses swirling in their wooden traps.
On the sea bed, Yoshitsune's jaw snaps open,

then closed. His carcass is a resting place
for minnows caught in the harum-scarum of war.

On Fancying American Film Stars

From the big screen, and larger than life for a week or two,
which is all a tangent universe can stand,
we take them home and introduce them to our modest living quarters.

Their baby blues stare out at us at all hours of the day and night,
prompting every manner of ridiculous thought, such as:
'The world is small', or 'What if Elvis could have taken to my mother?',

'I will ride across the desert on a purple roan, or some such,
for anything is possible', and even that old chestnut,
'There is only one for everyone alive.' The cat mewls

at its perpetually empty bowl, the work piles up on the desk,
but we simply say, with a new-found recklessness:
'This is not the most important thing in my life right now';

'you're a predator, catch your own'. We exist
in the bubble of our making, our souls glistening like celluloid,
by turns rock bottom and on fire. What causes it to disappear?

Who can know, but one day we double-take to find ourselves
filing them away in the rack of lost hopes,
with the show-jumping videos and 'twelve easy tunes for classical
guitar',

the cat purring as it settles on the easy chair, as if to say
'What then, what then', the sky sucking back its thunder-claps
and storm winds, saving only one small cloud, which loiters there,

putty grey, shedding rain like tiny lead balloons
on the pristine terraces. And somewhere else a universe explodes.

Interface

Mary-up-the-road is having it out with Margaret-down-the-way
as to who's the bigger fucker. *You! No you are!*
I challenge even you to sleep through this. Your limbs splay
over the square of bed that's 'my side', encroaching like a star-

fish, wriggling in ever deeper to the sand
as Mary has it out with Margaret-down-the-way
and kids rattle up the pavement like a jug band
knocking every other door for Matthew, is Matthew coming out
        to play.

They smile sweetly when I say: He doesn't live here.
Momentarily you snuffle, and rise for tea,
then I lose you to the depths again. Your breath gutters

like a stuck pig's, your eyelid leaks an underwater tear.
There is havoc at the gallery, you say, taking
my wrist. And *Plato's on the riverbed*. Then you roll over without
        so much as a 'Help me'.

Affliction

One hand medicates the other. Fierce lovers
who cannot face the world beyond their empathy –
the dishes are a cross-Atlantic trawl, the crush
of another hand as painful as the loss of self –
they spend their mornings with a tube of hydrocortisone
coating themselves in greasy layers,
neat strips of elastoplast like gauze for the soul.

Their weakness is beyond compare:
mere spatterings of weather send them running for relief;
they have the bearded woman's reticence, moist fears
and raptures make them weep under their skin.

Their involuntary breakdowns – crack-lipped
extrusions in the face of the simplest task –
amaze the capable amongst them,
who have long since ceased to run for tissues,
to proffer themselves.

Nights see them chart
a lonely course on the bus home – excitable, avoiding
the fabrics, they may once forget themselves
and reach for the button with an agonising, blossoming wrench.

They reject the shower experience, making straight
for the bedroom where they lurk, as under igneous rock,
in the shadow of a freshly laundered pillow-case.

Neighbours marvel at their honeymoon period,
which never seems to phase: their grief and trust alike
are inexplicable, their lush hibernations brief
as pin-hole apertures, the toss-up over seasons.

Medusa

Dance, oddity, savouring your element,
in the two-tone shallows of the pier
where water slops the earth and each is negligent,
uncertain of its goal; where the sun whisks patterns over dark hills,
each stone, for seconds at a time, ablaze,
and everything is tempted by its opposite,
by this unsteadiness of soul. Pig-
headedness has carried you, curiosity like a dusky wave,
from the sea's deep innards where the trawlermen
pass by with irises of salt, sea-brains accepting without question
what the sea herself pronounces difficult, all
circus tent and tinsel, a shape to which she cannot put her name.
You are uglier than beautiful,
your long legs trailing you like afterthoughts
tacked on by the children of the moon, by those
who cannot leave as well alone
the pure thing but must meddle with it, cross-wise;
harsh queen of Copydex and stick-pins,
you are nothing to the purpose,
made flesh by that rebellious god.
The waters spin you like a dirty jewel: flushed out
to crusty deaths on beaches
or retained in the darkest of her vaults, the sea
would have you seem a thing of nowheres; soft spume
of unconsidered thought, she is tarrying for time
with you, dabbling for ways to rein you in.
But the sun makes honeycombed your playground
and your body pirouettes through gold-splashed avenues
lazily surveying what is there, your slow limbs tickling
at the borderline between two worlds of sound...
You can hold me here for how long?
We are neither of us of this and my instep aches
to be away, the tide is coming back for you
but come, curio, and dance with me a moment longer:
let us run aground together
in this piebald territory of waiting
where bits and pieces fasten into grace.

Tinkerness

(in memory of George Best)

Something in the way you man that ball
is endemic to this city.
As you spoon it down the field
you are both barbarian and ballet-
girl: as rough and ready as they come, with a zing
that's ever-so-slightly off the mark.
I can almost hear you saying:
'That thing's as hard as a hoor's heart'
to the notion that something might be fragile,
the injunction to take care
as you blaze seamlessly from goal to goal,
and, latterly, disaster to disaster,
taking life one dance-step at a time,
never thinking of the future, each move
an explosion of your love. A love,

perhaps, that also carried, even in its prime,
a fair share of that 'drug-dull fatalism' ascribed to us;
that had taken from the red-brick terraces of east
Belfast more than anyone could fathom
from the flick of your fleet feet. Snow looms
in the grey sky of your maiden city on this cold
November afternoon, and they interrupt the run of the radio
as you have always interrupted plans,
diving in when you were least expected,
a blur of energy kitted out in black and white and red.
You were the fierce alembic of your homeland,
your dream-runs down and round the Cregagh Road
going on to render you ambassador, to wide worlds,
of a certain sideways motion: the last, perverse twist;
quips tailor-made in this city of oddments.

SARAH JACKSON

Sarah Jackson was born in 1977, grew up in Berkshire and now lives in Brighton. She is currently completing a DPhil in Creative and Critical Writing at Sussex University. Her poetry has been published in a wide range of anthologies and journals including *The Rialto*, *Magma*, *Envoi*, *New Writer*, *Interpreter's House*, *Other Poetry* and *Booklight*. Her debut pamphlet, *Milk* (Pighog Press, 2008), was shortlisted for the first Michael Marks Award for Poetry Pamphlets. In 2008 she took part in a writing residency on the Fielding Programme near Glasgow, was given a 'show-case' in *Magma*, and her poems were awarded prizes in the Kent and Sussex and Wigtown Poetry competitions. Sarah has taught creative writing in psychiatric settings, in schools, and at undergraduate and postgraduate level. She is poetry editor of *New Writer* magazine.

Vanishing Twin

For years, I've hid
in a cracked hotel
tipping the moors:

I sleep days, among piles
and piles of laundry;
nights, I steal dreams

wrap them up
in soft white towels
longing for you

my duck egg girl
my vanishing twin.
Do you remember me?

I still feel the ache
of your lidless space
your imprint on my skin.

Two Mothers

One just crawled into my cot,
laid her head in my lap,
I'm tired, she said.
I stroke gin-caked lips,
sweep away the hair that cracks her cheek.
Her old eyes close;
I smile, hold onto her head,
gather her to me
as dark walks past the window.

I have another mother below
who is cleaning walls, singing,
her tight, white hips spinning,
while this one sleeps.

Too big for my bed
she's a coal sack leaking milk,
skirts mashed between slumped legs,
hands huge, wider than my face.
Her arm falls out of the cot,
too fat to fold back. She won't wake
and though toothless I bite her.
I don't mean to make her cry.

There's not room for us both,
and cold, hairless, hungry
I slip through the bars easily.
Though I have two mothers
neither hears me climb in
with the boneless dolls,
close the toy-box lid.

What Daddy Built

That night the dogs cried again and woke you.
Wanting to be still-small, you climbed inside the doll's house
that daddy built. Sunk below your bed line, it waited, floored.

In the darkness your bed was a long, hard road
and you belly-crawled on all fours as if you were still a baby.
Hem rucked around your gut, you were naked under a pale purple
          nightie,

your bare bum smiling up at the moon as you crept;
your big-girl body a white worm, big-girl skin rubbing nylon;
static cracking up the dark with tiny forks of yellow,

like yellow boned fingers with long yellow nails
and where your big-girl bed fell away steeply you dropped to the floor.
The dogs cried again and blind, you reached out, found the house

that daddy built. You stroked its door, finger-felt its floor,
placed your cheek on glossy gables. You ran your tongue-tip
all up the walls; bit down, the wood splinters sweet, cool.

You licked the shiny red roof and it was so slick it slid nearly
deep inside you. Truly, you could eat this doll's house that daddy built,
or it could eat you. And then you unhooked the door, reached inside

to touch the doll people, the length of your white arm
folding right into its hot red belly. Finally you slept,
your head in the kitchen window, a daddy doll in your teeth.

Leftovers

The second Saturday of every month
they remind me how to work the remote,
point out the rocket salad with walnut and blue cheese,
kindly suggesting I don't touch
the thermostat or the baby.
Then they go to friends' for dinner
or to that nice little Thai place on the corner
of Bridge Street, just the two of them.

Watching *Casualty* on wide-screen
I thumb through last year's holiday snaps,
left out under the solicitor's letter.
I side-step the salad but sip Sauvignon blanc
from an open bottle,
eat Cheerios out of the packet,
fat fingers greasy with spit.
At a quarter to, I check the baby
is breathing.
Watching him feels like spying
and I sit on stripped pine floors,
pretending it's all mine.

They rattle the keys as a warning.
Warmed by wine she offers me a drink,
insists I stay.
We can have a proper chat over breakfast, she says.
Yes, she says, as she always does, do stay.
In the spare room, I undress, wait,
listen for the sounds of them breathing.

Night hums softly,
and by dawn my legs are wound around
the white silk of her wedding gown.

The Instant of My Death

The bus was crammed and the fat man rubbed against my leg like
    a damp cat
while you read *The Jataka Tales* three rows from the back

and we all stumbled on; wheels and hours grinding, tripping
as Spiti rose up around us, sky propped open by its peaks.

I traced the rockline on the window with my finger,
counted cows and gompas, felt my eyes glaze over

until we reached Gramphoo. There, where the road divided,
I saw a thin boy in red flannel squat between two dhabas;

a black-eyed bean, slipped-in between two crags, he was so small
that I almost missed him, until he turned, gap-toothed, and shot me

with a toy gun. And a piece of me stopped then, though the bus
    moved on,
and the fat man beside me cracked open an apple with his thumb.

Footing

The earth is soft
and I am sinking.
Beneath the mountain

the Chinese keep
engineered diseases
and black tanks.

Days pass without sign.
It is silent except
for water, aeroplanes.

Hours I do not sleep,
watch the submarines
slip by down there

like titanium eels.
Some days I smell
anthrax in the trees.

Clam

The beach at night is my body.
You taught me this,
and how goose barnacles
will slit your wrists
if you're not careful.

Tonight I'm fused with clams.
They stick upright like my sister's
fingernails or bunches of car keys
and when I try to run away from myself
they slice the soles of my bare blue feet.

I've never seen so much water:
it sluices through my bones
like your sperm, your spit,
its cold crawling up inside me
coming home in my chest.

You taught me about molluscs too;
how they have tongues for feet,
kill dog whelks
by tethering them to rock
until they starve to death.

You always find me;
dragging me out of the sea again,
the water pours out of me again;
your boots snapping the clams
like children clapping.

ANNIE KATCHINSKA

Annie Katchinska was born in Moscow in 1990 and has lived in London for most of her life. She was brought up on a diet of Russian folk songs and 90s pop music. In 2006 she was one of the Foyle Young Poets of the Year – the winners went on to start *Pomegranate*, an online zine publishing poets under 30, which Annie helps out with very, very sporadically. She came second in the Christopher Tower Poetry Competition in 2007, and has had poems published in *Magma* and *Mimesis*. Her Faber New Poets pamphlet is forthcoming in 2010. She is currently studying classics at Cambridge.

Crash

OK OK OK *listen.* You mincepied? You roastpotatoed? You goose-
    fatted?
You burping in public? No worries, no worries, come, come and see
what we have here. We have Lycra, pink, green, leopard-print,
and pumping pumping muzak (top 40 type, you'll recognise),
gym membership, yoga mat, swimming costume, Lucozade coupons
et cetera now: listen: carefully: you start and you do not
stop you do not stop look LOOK at her, she did not stop
now look at her bouncy hair and happy children
and the sunlight. No worries, come, come.
If you got the money buy berries, porridge, bulgur wheat,
this exotic polysyllabic lettuce that actually consumes fat inside you
or if not, percentages, 3%, 1%, 0%, or traffic light colours.

Sooper-dooper. Nothing you couldn't work out with a piece of paper
and a brain and some time but never mind this is prettier.
This is Comic Sans. This is louder. Come, come.
OK OK OK go. We have our cake. See you next year.

Bergamot

Not tonight, at least. Not tonight. Now turn your spine
to plainsong, turn the mainlight off, and shut the door

on the evening's fried buttery food. Time yourself only
to a kettleclick, pour it, stir out the day,

let it darken like a wandering angel. And breathe
in bergamot, the juice of brittle leaves you want

to press against your head, or weave into a dress
in which to rustle on dry lightning nights.

You echo too much, like the fox refusing
to die outside among all the market's

aging meatcrumbs and fruit. Drink,
burn away your lips. When you cup this hot planet

and hear it turn, you're that rare thing,
a listener. Let moths flood the market

and chew up your city, you're going nowhere tonight.
Not tonight. A scrap of fox whimpers,

cooling its cheeks with old plastic.
Grapes rot softly on string.

February

Tight, tight skin, and the room rings. It matters.

This is February, so she dissolves
smiley faces of vitamin C in oceanic
glasses of water, eyeballs herself and thinks

tendon

tetanus

optic nerve

and someone visits and juggles everything in the fruitbowl
even the grapes, but she binds her face

in white scarves, smears marjoram on her hands. Her
eyes are stethoscopes, her lungs
broken harmonicas, she sees

each minute as a grain of brown rice

laid out on a table, death locked
in scummy bones and staggers
upstairs to Google *–osis, –osis!*
join the dots between

her skin crackling under cotton, rattling
beneath bracelets of eczema, camel-shaped bruises, bitter moths
and the dirt on the window –

the world glows, glows.
Watch her
check her fingertips for flames.

Too Many Storms

Often, pretending to sleep, I hear my father
in the next room, importantly flicking his books.

Sometimes he hums –
a song from the summer he said he'd hung a thousand wind
chimes
in high places, dark places my eyes could never reach –

He hasn't been himself.
He says there are too many storms on this island,
not enough elsewhere. He won't explain this word,
insists I learn to play chess then snaps
that I hold the king too tightly
and scatters the pawns. I sweep up bewildered ivory.
Now he walks among the trees, kicking all the foliage;
now he's taken to wearing robes
of boiling velvet, whirlpools of blue. He kneels by the shore,
his hands running through bright shells,
half-weeping over the clockwork tides,
promising freedom to the air.

I read his books in secret,
thumb the pencil-scratched footnotes
he keeps me awake with. In them,
children have wings, monsters are conquered
by other monsters, men who look like my father
line their wrists with stars and everywhere

there is furious physics,
a sense of time running out,
talk of splintering ships.

Toni Braxton

My fate was a weird surname and lipstick that glowed in the dark,
and adults who slurred, 'Russia! Russsssia!' at video cameras every
year. My parents pinned carpets to the walls and bought a tape
recorder, gave me bad asthma attacks with Beverley Craven, Ace
of Base, Enya, more Enya. Crawling around under the table at
dinner parties retrieving furry gherkins and measuring guests' legs
with a tape measure, I thought Red Square was full of onions and
we'd never go home, and I wanted karaoke not two alphabets, a
frog in my throat like Toni Braxton or the woman from M People.
The song played simultaneously on Capital, Heart and Magic until
one day I heard she had to stop begging her heart to be unbroken or
her boobs would explode, true story I swore, as somebody's parents
filed for divorce and somebody else burst into tears in another room
saying they only ever talked to carpets, by now drooping off the
walls in a tragic fashion and smelling of gherkins. Say you love me.

Fairytale

You called. 'I just threw my folder
out the window. Come over.' So I blink against a night
of carousels, of children clutching hymnbooks and pound coins
and crying over gingerbread, your handwriting
of '*this – this –*' skidding along the pink pavement
under a sky snagged in scattered Latin.
Let's live and love, you say, live and love more
only look at these toadstools lodged in my chest, look
at my hair, heavy and skimming the ground.
I stand on your street. You want every winter
to be a fairytale, 'But there are mirrors,' I whisper,
'apples, the year will be filled with tricks.'
Turn off your light; feel this air between us; feel it
thick with spinning wheels.

Labyrinths

They sweep the hair off the tracks. It's a living –
the tunnels lined with wispy human carpets
connecting Angel to Old Street, Oval to Kennington;
and the walk home, chilly in a dawnbreak
of skin and eyelashes. Learning to see
the world of losses – weekends that finish with
scraped-away lips, street goddesses with grand piano laughs
and not enough toes, nails slammed in doors, teeth
on tabletops.
      And dreams of turning in the serpentine dark,
peering through tangled clouds: holding up brown, red, blonde
handfuls, to cry, 'Look, you left this at Blackfriars, you
who stand there on – what is it now? – Thursday morning, who never
give yourselves to strangers, not in sharp electric light of day.
Can you hear me? Are you OK?'

Peach

Juice soaks the sculpted horses' mouths. The men
rising from the foams are catching coins
between their teeth, beneath the morning fruit
that drips the day across each roof and turns
our scalps as pink as ham. Wine on my chin.
My feet pulped into dust. The armless boys
and dogs who sweat in corners, starving girls
who eat their packs of postcards. Waving air.
She said that sun was her sarcophagus,
she told us we should walk and walk. Too poor
for ice-cream, suncream, gulping in the ghosts
of whores and triumphs, turning to the ball
that sings the way exploding fruit will sing.
Just dare. You'll only ever see this once.

MARK LEECH

Mark Leech was born in 1977 in Newcastle-under-Lyme, Staffordshire, and grew up there. After several years in London – which led to his long-poem sequence *London Water*, published by Flarestack – he now lives in Oxford with his wife and daughter. He won the Stephen Spender Prize for poetry in translation in 2004, and some of his translations make up the chapbook *The Anglo Saxon Elegies*, published by Piper's Ash, and the virtual chapbook *Selected Poems* by Lorca, at Brindin.com. His poems and translations have appeared in a wide range of magazines, including *The Wolf*, *nthposition.com* and *Modern Poetry in Translation*.

Hobgoblin Gate

Glob light fat in the sky   late heat's smell
sinking root deep
Last year's leaves   first of night
                  she waits, not buried
not forest   waits   as concrete waits
for water's finger to push
split it, run white grains
down the valley bottom
Wound in branches breath a fly foot on her tongue's edge
unseen   Steps crack round her head
   walkers muttering

the path shadows them up   She still   still
lips tight as bound twigs − keep her second life
in   no longer binding fortune
over hope
                    The path's half moon cups her
hunches her down   onto her name

− − −   − − − −

Too named by kind and place   This is her
overripe, bird raddled
                This sun-sink hour walkers slip
pause   red moon up   rooks calling sleep
A car talks under trees
She bites her solid lips one lit house in her mirror eye
Better to leave (for towns' safe alleys
warm waste from kitchens)
                            But she's
in the leaf pile stubborn as bone
eyes out for stars
                She waits −
one night something fire will come
through wood and dark   press itself
in her   trunks and branches crack

It rushes hungry out toward the gate

The Tumulus Mutters

Lump of a ghost,
like the scalp of a god hill hooded.
        In rain I soften
                        and any searching arms
could thrust my grasstop through
for the root-webbed passageways
down to gold-dressed bones:
        the treasured myth of whitebeards
        photographed among their labourers.

                      The land is my haunting.
In the sheets of winter,
in the tautening of fog
your tarmac, phantoms,
walker,
your guiding hedgerows, mirage:
now mark the pathways and prayerways,
stoneways and cattleways,
            the battle ways
of the valley's cauldron.
They live under me,
blood corned
like every English field.

Oil

Dante, *Purgatory*, canto XIX, *ll.* 1-36

When day had given up the world
to the hard moon, thrashed by Earth
or Saturn, or some other punisher

the hour that prophets foretell the rising
of great stars out east down roads
that flare with falling shells

a woman came staggering to me
eye pained, foot bound, hands
yellowed with a cancer.

My gaze upon her membraned flesh
jerked her straight, as from a morgue
her tongue slopping free

her body stiff like one about to fall.
Her face washed in a flood of colour –
some lust, or blood, had burst its banks.

So her story was released, and she
keened a note that held me closer
than any prayer-built hope:

'I the Siren, sweet in my throat
sweet on the sea, bring crude men
to ruin, spilt on rocks and currents.

Wandering Ulysses was trapped in my slick:
any man who's burned for me is caught –
no engine can undo my grip.'

At her pause a lady, cold, stepped
between us. Her icy breath thinned
the Siren's spell to air, invisible.

'She's got him! He's bending to her lips!'
My guide was closing in, eyes fixed
on her white shroud. He grabbed the Siren

and laid her open, the belly slack
stinking, choking me, waking me
with poisoned air. My eyes fell

on my guide. 'Three times I've called on you
to wake!' he said. 'Now rise: this path
will take us on to lighter skies.'

Thames Border

*The forts at Wittenham and Dorchester. In prehistory,
a fertile valley made men as rich as oil does now.*

Land scarred with a man's mark:
our kill acknowledged.
　　Each heft of earth ground in the throat
like the heft of a blade in the charge.
The great defences rose as slow
as the last wound's numbness.

                    Over the river
over ramparts we see figures
leaning on spears, stained stakes
jerking smoke.
They call edge spirits out.

Ours cluster in grass, among cattle.
The river snorts her drunkenness,
evening trickling from her mouth.

    Listen, concentrate, keep the crows
spread evenly from them to us.
            There's peace then, the sort
that keeps a man angry,
touching his hand to his knife,
looking on enemy ground.

Dracul

Harmless – as a game of arrows –
he strums an uneasy waltz
on the tuned streets.

Self origamic, he ducks
the cabman's backward glance,
black sack on the floor at dawn.

Wear his shoulder's thrust
a red outrage on your arm
down escalator, up escalator, home.

The bed a sweatslick,
his raid a drunken street fight's yell
staked through your sleep.

The heart sobs to his persuasions
that you – you! –
are his dear victim.

A plausible salesman. Pluck out his teeth.

Snowfall in Woodland

There's a curve that promises
swift return to the glossy road, but the printless way
  is set with fear, the nothing in the trees
                  I turn my head towards –

         The snow comes in in comets blanking out
spring's solitary flag of petals
among the cold-stripped twigs   No trespass   No treaty

The path fades   Behind,
a glimpse of silent field
frosted and alone
The printless way is set with fear, the nothing in the trees
               I turn my head towards –

a tribal memory of torches
weaving unstable nets of light,
the blistering *huff* of a dog on the trail
             the men who follow

Aftertaste

Bullying, the sky, long views from the road
cut low by dropping sun, the cables black cracks
to slip and mutter through, saying here the leaves
are done, a foot rubs mud from the ground
the hill soaks, grumbling, and where houses sit
seasons are finished, doorframes gummed
with damp, fibreoptics crammed with speech,
taking the phone from its bed will flood the cold
room with summers and wars and what better
than to leave it still, go to the window, stare
at black lines distancing, the top of the car
dusted with remnants of weather, time falling,
the whole lit world in another valley
while here dark rises, autumn stopped in it, night.

January Common

Too cold for toadstools
   orange smudges on stained wood
   white caps flat in the pale grass
the new year entombed

We talk about the future
wind teeth on the rims of our ears

a hundred words like ours
patter like dogs round frozen pools
   turn back following children
      down grey avenues   out of hearing

Too cold for toadstools
the frost sews them up
snaps their stems

trees thin as hairs
             bow over soil-black leaves

No better time to kiss

TOBY MARTINEZ DE LAS RIVAS

Toby Martinez de las Rivas was born in 1978. He grew up in Somerset then moved to North-East England to study history and archaeology at Durham. He first worked as an archaeologist and this, together with the landscape of Northumberland and the work of North-East writers such as Barry MacSweeney and Gillian Allnutt, have had a significant impact on the development of his own poetry. He won an Eric Gregory Award in 2005 and the Andrew Waterhouse Award from New Writing North in 2008. His Faber New Poets pamphlet is published in October 2009. He currently lives in Gateshead where he teaches English to asylum seekers and refugees.

The White Road

I

for Mary Bullen, memoryless

> *Name the constellations for us,*
> *The tracks they drag through the night*
> *Like a hawk's mind stripping a rat*

Beneath the holed roof showing stars
    rats run through the attic,
rock back on haunches whispering
    into a spread fan of claws,
or scamper with swift, witless intent
    up the tattered remainders,
the slashed fabrics peed on, despoiled.

On the high days, Father Enright spoke
    about the primal self: how
it was like a rat one had to tame – hands
    in gloves, a string about its
neck – to break it in the house of its flesh.

II

> *'You are spinning,' I said to her. Her eyes glanced over me,*
> *making no effort of attention.*
> *'Yes,' she said.*
>
>   D.H. LAWRENCE, Twilight in Italy

Marquesa of the torched estate,
    ascend the trap in sudden poverty,
settle your skirts, smooth them
    on the seat and wait most patiently.

Confusion rules all the desolate.
    The flogged and the footloose ruin
the house, tear hangings down.
    You are left with your Sunday best.

They have nailed your husband
    to the branches of the ragged oak,
and the lamb has changed places
    with the tiger, nothing is as it was.

Time flows beyond reckoning.
    There, there, pat my hands, my head,
your eyes vacated, blank glass
    where, occasionally, a child pauses.

Is it the rat of the body running
    blindly up tunnels, sniffing dead ends,
personality's armature unpicked
    twist by twist, disproving the gospels?

Set the trap in motion, harnessed
    to the world which turns a frightsome
eye to regard you over the meat
    of its shoulder, then turns to plod on.

At the juncture of the crosshatch,
    take the white road where the white
wind blows through white leaves
    and troubles your hair like wild garlic.

Take the white road where love
    is coterminous with flesh, unsupernal,
unlifted above the vesicle of its
    own surge and rush and failing like it.

Wave back without a smile, that's
    right, let the fingers do their own thing,
pluck at the lap aimlessly, remember
    the movements of crocheting or patch.

III

    Don't fret,
Mary Bullen, godcundnes is in the world.
    No cables of lightning fork
across your abyssal, graveyard of names
    and faces whose memory
rides off into an absence the size of a life.

    Mary, you were married in a chapel
near Versailles after the liberation.
    Jimmy drew it with pastels,
his despatch bike meeting its shadow
    on the whitewashed wall,
war-heavy like a warhorse broadsided,
    but attentive to each nudge
as he took off down the dappled lane
    in a roar of dust, what
a dish, past horses blown into trees
    with bits of half-track,
flesh and metal wind-chimes chiming,
    promising he'd be back
and good as his word.

    Godcundnes is in the world:
don't turn away from it. Don't turn away,
    as the kingfisher escapes the river
with its beakful of silver elvers,
    and the wren its thorny custody
in a flash of wings and black underbelly.

Poem, Three Weeks After Conception

The sky will be shaped like a bow when you crane your neck to pray
        into it.
Roofless, but not burned. Though black, spangled.

Your hair will be the white spray at High Force,
teeth pebbles in the vent.

You will escape the ogre of psoriasis that lives on the knees,
elbowcaps, genitals and face.

For you the stars have already locked into place.

For you the blue coltsfoot in the allotment will be an electrical wonder.

The Red Kite, wolf and bear will return to the borders in numbers.

You will be buried in a country far away, a country like home,
of absolute rainfall.

Beneath a late moon, unfurling.

You shall witness the domination of Jerusalem.

The capsize of London.

I pray that I will never hit or humiliate you,
for whom the best wine in the world will be pressed in Kent.

Who will live to see supermarkets dictating military policy to governments.

Our Lady of Gateshead, watch over us.

from **Instructions on How to Raise the Dead**

brother, the king, knaves, the year the war ended, *p*liancy,   X
return, sophomore, repetition, furrow, the tower, rew*a*rds,
infancy, number of the beas*t*, kingdom, failsafe, paraclete,
her sc*e*nt, sarah, the rose, satan, falling leaves, power, lip,
bu*r*ned tree, the lamb, a cloud, halo, goshawk, sword arm,
loosestrife, the bear, ploughshare, they will *n*ever be able
to say, c*o*urt of the burning star, hand of peace, sorrow, to
love, bombsight, valley*s*, queen of hearts, false aspect, the
double image, the serpen*t*, a killing field, the rising moon,
trickery, haut*e*psalm, salted bacon, lorca, flowers, selfless,
the bee, *r*agged stone, the mouth is empty, the pin, primate,
white dove, positivism, skirmish, thank heaven, p*u*n, rame,
XVI   the world, the dragon, s*p*arrows, jeoffrey, bar, the burn, air,
watermint, the flesh, death, the wi*t*ch, a cloud, mercy, roan,
instruments of joie, the seat, fealty, my faraway, fie, en*o*ch,
n*i*neteen, asthenia cold, stop sign, the fool, mother of pearl,
the arrow, a little night music, cowardice, ba*n*g, black gold,
cremation, hedge of spears, qi, as the waves break, ora*t*ory,
a full t*e*n seconds later, tendernesse, hunting pike, relenting,
VII   the falstaff, w*r*ens, between her legs, the poets, rage, closed
XIV   doo*r*, falsehood, fire, the house of life is following after you

90

Twenty One Prayers for Weak or Fabulous Things

When animals which lived under water afterwards live in air, their
bodies change almost entirely, so as hardly to be known by any one
mark of resemblance to their former figure; as, for example, from
worms and caterpillars to flies and moths [...] These changes take
place in consequence of the unalterable rule, that the body be fitted
to the state [...] Now our present bodies are by no means fitted for
heaven.

WILLIAM PALEY,
Sermon XXVII, Of the State after Death

'I was once acquainted with a tall man,' he said to me at last, 'that
had no name either and you are certain to be his son and the heir
to his nullity and all his nothings.'

FLANN O'BRIEN,
The Third Policeman

As snow falls, as the first snow of this year falls & falls
    beyond all light & knowledge, I pray for Rufus
corrupted by blood parasites, whose liver is corrupted
    & whose eyes are uncorrupted by swivelling in
the weak light. I speak this prayer into the inflamed sun.

Secondly, I pray for stooping David who sees his dead
    sister walking in the bedroom each morning up
& down, a shadow of herself. I pray for all things that
    shed their skins: for snakes, for cicadas & silk
worms clasped to branches & hidden in rattling bushes.

Thirdly, I pray for a babbling drunk fisherman wearing
    no pants, dredged from the Tyne, who swore
everafter that by praying to Cuddy, he was able to call
    silver trout from the river, to throw themselves
from their element into his: & there they flop, gasping.

Fourthly, I pray for a war protester picketing the Sage,
    whose banner is stitched with cluster bombs
like falling seeds having the real viridian sting of black
    pansies opening. I pray for all things that open
& follow the sun, its star-track raked in the winter sky.

Fifthly, I pray for the ghost of Rene & the living ghost
  of Mary in the final blank stage of Alzheimer's,
nodding, clucking & fumbling. I pray for the sunflower,
  thin petals opening, head bowed, face nodding
imperceptibly nightward. It has arms, too, to hold itself.

Sixthly, I pray for a humble Yellowhammer who when
  he sings, sings in English, 'a little bit of bread
& no cheese.' This is acknowledgment of the body's
  need & the body's need to sing. I pray for the
ghost of Barry MacSweeney, which has a bird's throat.

Seventhly, I pray for the sparrow, tongue-cut, whirring,
  who in Egypt had a jackal's garish blunt head
& carried dead children across the river, but in England
  he's a merry fat fellow. I listen to his declining
brotherhood at Middlezoy: there is one fewer every day.

Eighthly, I pray for Jimmy who strokes Mary's hands &
  looks into Mary's empty shell each Wednesday,
also on her birthday & at Christmas. I pray for all things
  whose meat's scooped out. 8 is a sign of infinity
& also the sum of YHVH, double barrels of emptinesse.

Ninthly, I pray to the memory of the prodigious monster
  of Ravenna & prophesy with Arthur Clarke that
one day people will do away with their bodies & encode
  themselves as quanta or pure mental self-image.
The wing is for fickleness, the claw greed, the horn pride.

Tenthly, I pray for the last few seconds of a cold August,
  when the world is stilled, a sullen body of water
that brings forth flies & creeping beasts to my fingertips,
  my tongue a water-snail with soft horns poking
its head from between my lips, prince of dusk & muscle.

My eleventh prayer is for Migdale checking the hooves
  of his sheep for rot separating the hoof's heel,
sole & wall from their attachments to the foot, & for the
  sheep like amputees hobbling & nibbling at
lung flukes & brain worms: & some fall down, shaking.

My twelfth prayer is for the fledgling rooks shawled by
   ants beneath the nests. For the membra over the
black pods of their eyes. For their crackable elbows and
   white beaks. For the boot I bring down on them.
Let me love best of all the creeping things that creepeth.

My thirteenth prayer is for the memory of Nicholas Flüe
   who saw the face of the lord deformed by anger,
& whose own face was transformed into a deathmask by
   that vision of lacerations. He shuts his house to
light. *Today even the sparrows cannot bear to look at me.*

My fourteenth prayer is for psoriatics: for all the world is
   a clear mirror they fall apart in day after day, for
every beautiful thing grows to a scaly deformity & even
   the face of the sun glows scabrous & repugnant:
but like pythons they slough off their skins & slither out.

My fifteenth prayer is for you, Isabel, eaten by distance,
   I see the shape of your pumping heart & it is the
shape of the winter cherry shaken by a heave of wind, its
   blossom blows off, acquiescence in the bough,
but my heart is a bird high in the canopy: a false lapwing.

My sixteenth prayer is for the solitary writhing bee that I
   found in the allotment, like an aeronaut slumped
in the collapsed riggings of his machine: he thumped his
   sting once into the sodden ground to vent his fury
& is free to go. I am not free to go, nor will I be released.

My seventeenth prayer is to the memory of Christopher
   Smart kneeling in a cloud of honeybees at Stain-
drop to pray, or carving the Song to David into the walls
   at Bedlam with a workaday burin – a nail or key –
& with his fingertips rubbing charcoal into the scratches.

My eighteenth prayer is for the glass ghosts of Rudolf &
   Leo Blashka, combinations of moonlight & utile
organ, tendrils of pink glass hunting down their prey by
   security light and night vision: an inward ocean.
I say this prayer as the clouds shift to smother the moon.

My nineteenth prayer is for that one who sat in watch on
     the top stair when the child came home, to guard
against the visit of the devil, whose raw stare counteracts
     supernatural malice and who, after the dragon &
the owl, is the most canny & puissant of all living beasts.

My twentieth prayer is cobbled from nineteen fragments:
     four of flesh, two of wood, one is a shred of paper
from which a peregrine takes wing: another is its falling.
     Ten are made of air & the eighth means nothing.
There is a gap between each one where the breath comes.

Lastly, I pray for the makers of prayers, which are poems
     we say to ourselves in the hard times, cold times,
dry times, tucked in tenements & tower blocks, in the lock-
     ups of our bodies, between the soil & sky, falling
& falling like snowflakes beyond all light & knowledge.

The First Appearance of the Angel of Death, in His Aerial Form

Terror, I remember where I saw you first: on a cliff-edge
Above Milford Haven, all the grass yellow with buttercups
Bar at the black entrance to an antique ferro-concrete pillbox
Where endless traipsings corrupted the earth into a wet splurge.

You reared up above the cliff, your belly sleek and grey,
I fell into that square black slot and fainted clean away.
With a *ha ha ha* and a *ho ho ho*, my father brought me round,
My eyes were anchored in the dark, my body to the ground.

O, that was the summer of my father's father's passing,
The policeman with a face like the picture of a policeman's face
Waiting in the whiteness of the door and my father repeating
He's gone? He's gone? and so he had, to a silentswaying place.

The summer the swept-winged and beroundled Vulcan roared
And the yellow grass and everything and I fell into darkness.

JONATHAN MORLEY

Jonathan Morley was born in 1979 in the south of England and lives in Coventry. He is the founder and editor of the Heaventree Press in that city and is a PhD researcher in Caribbean literature at the University of Warwick. As an editor, his current and forthcoming books include a new edition of Sir Walter Ralegh's *Discoverie of Guiana* (1596), the *Collected Early Poems of Derek Walcott*, and *Geminar*, an anthology of younger British poets in Portuguese translation. He received an Eric Gregory Award in 2006, and his debut pamphlet of poems, *Backra Man*, was published in 2008, together with a jazz album, *Backra Men*.

Iberian Baroque
Igreja de São Francisco, Porto

Aztec or Inca, I stare granite-eyed
from an arch of grey stone. Wreaths
of stone flowers curve in the arch
whose foot is on my head. No gold.
Other heads are set about me,
animals: *Beaver*, from Labrador,
Yaguara, from the January River:
larger than mine, my head was shrunk
to allow for the enlarged earlobes.
No gold on this stone totem.

Around, beyond the chain of the arch
everything is gold: heaven,
I saw this scrawl on shields of mashed feathers
when Quetzalcoatl, feathered snake
appeared from the East as a bearded man;
heard it uttered when my father
was given a feather, chained in a circle
of dirt and made to fight snake-men
with fangs of steel: commend thy soul.

Windward, through waves of gold,
five men are beheaded, in Morocco:
one – *desculpe* – neck snapped like tulip,
two: hair in fist of turbaned warrior,
all round-eyed, staring at the gold,
futile poor martyrs of Morocco.

Somewhere diagonal, blind:
another head, not like mine
peers from the root of a tree
where are hung many ghosts,
at its tip, a woman in blue
cradling a child's body. The head
with round cheeks of a child
supports the weight of tree, and above
a child-tribe clusters gold-gold
though some have smouldered, blackened
sad in smoke of years, and below:

the roots of the place are marble,
white roots as of mountain
and even in its caverns
skulls are scarred like trophies
gleaming in the ink-black
chattering through trapdoors
down to the dried-up bilges
and shifting floor of bones.

For Lee Miller

In the bleak washroom,
its motel-cramp, your elf's face
cynical, tired. The metronome
poised below your eyes, a demoiselle
out of Picasso, the glow dimmed
that has flooded the darkrooms
of uncounted hearts, luminous one.
The little Führer watches you bathe
from his frame on the bath's corner, fist
at his hip, chest thrust out;
often he must have stood
to attention in the shower,
practising faces, the pipes applauding
DA DA dada dada   DAA DAA dada dada –
you'll write for *Vogue* that the place is
well-stocked with wines and whiskeys,
for a teetotaller: Berchtesgarten.
Heated walls, you wired back in June
from Cologne, and the bloody, clawed handmarks
of the roasting victims baked like the designs
on pottery. The inhabitants must have known.
Now steam mars his pristine grey tiles:
a ghost of fingerprints near the tap.
Pierrot completes the set.
Facing him, on a polished table
a foot-high nude stroking her stone-blonde hair,
elbow mimicking your elbow's gesture
for washing a collarbone, alabaster.
And do your triptych of faces consciously echo
that threesome you described as the hangover
to a great party you just missed in Leipzig:
in one of the offices, a grey-haired man
at his desk with head bowed
on crossed hands; sprawled in a chair
his faded wife, a stitch of blood down her chin;
dusty nurse-daughter with pretty teeth
stretched on the sofa in dreamless sleep?
that SS guard you snapped, his face
moon-white beneath the glass canal?

Her breasts and stomach are waxen, bulge
like yours in those maddening photographs
taken by your Pygmalion father
when you were twenty-one.
Your boots queue like men:
fecit Hitler's bathmat with the Dachau mud.

Coventry Boys

As when the Africans
dropped seeds from a bag
they were bringing home
one sunday
all along the road
emerald fists
bust up the tarmac

for three days
was festival
melon rinds and kiwi skins
heap plastic spoons
sound systems speaking
community

now the Indian fireworks
banging for weeks
princesses delivered home
wrapped in darkness

tinfoil leaves
dervish at the corner-shop
scurf from sky's anvil

*

one pie-shaped boy
in sky-blue T
jumps from the car's
passenger door
to flob on bus

while his father's
hid by the bus,
almost knocks me

*

three rat-face boys
playing cricket:
foot-length of dowel
fistful of gravel
end of the road

*

six little Sikhs
pelt like foals
uphill from Swanswell –
their heads are boats,
the sky scrap metal

*

name
Arthur Genders
Builders Merchants
off Clovelly Row
Kev's Chop Shop
Beautiful Cuticles
the Sky Bleu Batch Bar
Moira's Wet Fish
the city names
the sanctuary
of those who turn the lathes
those who drive the buses
those who make fins
that spin the propellors
to fly the jet engines
rolling the king
back to his boys
those who make screws
of certain length
and are sold along
with their machine
those who mend

great leather belt
hundreds of yards
on the factory floor
to synchronise the men
the screeching and strafing of metal
thing strange in these days

        *

above the Skydome
of Martin Brown's head
borrowed in foam
replacing the old
Locarno Ballroom
as the new home
of Central Library
in the late Observer
a ballerina
tries out a new move
in silhouette
against a lit window
lifting an ankle
up to her temple
raising her arms
like the Cross of Nails
while outside the credit crunch
empties old Spon St
and Martin Brown reads
a poem for children
on being animals
it is written
then a man comes in
closes the curtains
as darkbright october
brings autumn to winter

        *

I'll take you, love, up the Ollybrush Balti
and I will buy you chicken jahlfrezi,
we'll listen to the radio all night long
its mingle of Bollywood and Quran
and I'll ignore the intercom's commands
for your eyelashes curl like their melodies:

the only way to travel, beetling down
the Hill, the drilling engine shouts to roar
then we're swooping like Whittle on the town,
panels shaking, the tom-tom's crosshairs trained
upon the point our chariot was born
as precise as German radio-beams
flickring along our moonlit rivers:
the Burges – the Birdcage – the Campbell – Club Release,
and what of the abuse, the vomit-stained
seat, quick-legged lads in the entry, the
Poles encroaching on the licensed strip?
I carry a kirpan, and at my call
each sore-arsed cabbie in the Foleshill Road
will be at my back, nimbler than the police
whose cast-off gadgets our quick sons can doctor.

An Outing
(for David Dabydeen)

Bank oliday. Cun thought e ws clevoo,
varyin th way he walk work
bt party sez he's weak, like wimmin,
decreed no snaketongue willevoo fit
on our unswervin ancien *p*ath
frm gettinna girl pregnun pub n funeral

n mighty is th man bring traitors funeral
n silvoo th spray offa car, so we work
east like angels alonga wet ribbon've *p*ath.
Bully sez tho sisterfuckoo circumcise wimmin.
I remember 'sistoo – she ws fit,
would've liked kissin oo, bt she ws clevoo

like those eastern bastards mus thing they're clevoo
b4 2 cov kids X their *p*ath.
Most've town ws dead's a funeral
bt pub full've loudmouthes, hot fer wimmin:
Cun isn' arahnd, gone awhy on work,
bt u could try is daad, yeah mate, quite fit.

101

Bully ws strong, n happy's dogs fit
onna hare, kickin Daad into path
wiv boots like cars fer the ol man's funeral.
World like a watch, nevoo knowna day's work,
CUN should KEEP is TRAP SHUT, fing they're fckink-'levoo,
Say this fer Daad: e squeak like wimmin

n radio returnin full've anxious men
at latest woe frm some raqi misfit.
Saw sky ahead bt behin black's work.
We sat silent, couln't think've anythink-'levoo.
Valholl is full, fuck-off back yr funeral
bt ow can I be lost, nowon ever lit my path?

Betterer fullbelly thanna windin path
n Bully, that bastard, mus be gettink-'levoo
fer e downed is pint, home-to-be wiyis wimmin
thru th dark narroo terraces where we fit
n summoo breathe sadness, quiet's a funeral
bt I'm off seeka whore thj star' work!

Issa funeral is work
bt u take fit wimmin
by path t'r clevoo.

Dobeš' Snail
Muzeúm Milana Dobeša, Bratislava

Take concentric rings
bisect
     bisect
          bisect
& remove   carefully   the
most of them.   Replace
the last arcs   in pastel shades,
peach   coral   olive   mud,   enamels
of the snail. All –   meticulous,   unto tippexing
your starting dots
     white now
     where the paper yellows.

              Dobeš saw shapes
                              with a snail's motion
              later, stalked or bulging metalworks
              mirroring only pen –
    those uneven geometries,
    their snail-lunge.

Such natural shapes from
              metal, glass –
the inkblot expanding on the filter
moiré of concentric rings
printed on glass fronting
concentric rings printed
on metal –   zebzagging segments spiking
towards circle's centre,
                              its snail.

Saunter round the crevices of his house,
at gallery pace: andante, and
as in a late summer yard
raking the leaves
the bull snail who, last time you looked, was still
yet has limed many inches, and by its silver signature,
not straightly
shrinks into its whorl –   just so
              the inkblot splurging –   then gone –
trickery –   a bicoloured rod
                    fluorescent plastics
                              mounted in a half-sphere mirror.

    – vaginal ripple of its foot –

Matisse, on his deathbed,
tearing crêpe   into bold chunks: snail,

          this one –   different,
                    an illusion of spiral;

downstairs...

          mechanical chomping of jaws around the leaf,
          googled in spheres of foil   the creature's eyes.

103

ADAM O'RIORDAN

Adam O'Riordan was born in Manchester in 1982. He read English at Oxford University and later won a scholarship to study under Andrew Motion at the University of London, where he was awarded the inaugural Peters Fraser and Dunlop Poetry Prize. In 2006 he received an Arts Council England Writers' Award. In 2008 his pamphlet *Queen of the Cotton Cities* (tall-lighthouse) won an Eric Gregory Award. He is co-editor of *The Shape of the Dance*, the selected prose of Michael Donaghy. In 2008 Adam became the youngest ever Poet-in-Residence at The Wordsworth Trust, the Centre for British Romanticism in Cumbria. He writes regularly on poetry and language for guardian.co.uk.

NGC3949

a galaxy in Ursa Major whose formation mirrors,
almost exactly, that of our own.

Back from the perforated dark and growing distance,
Hubble's milky image brings us to ourselves.

The echo pitched up from the moss-wet well:
a lover's shape, that indelible stain on the iris.

(Years down the line, you swear blind
the cut and sway of a dark form is her.

Neon dazzles the rain-slicked street
as you wave away the cab and push

back down through the crowd into the bar,
pilot charting the wrong star by candlelight,

leagues off course, the face, of course, is another's.)
In this spiral galaxy the arms embrace the core.

Not her – or your idea of her – and never will be.
It doesn't matter how beautiful your guess is.

Manchester

Queen of the cotton cities,
nightly I begin to piece you back into existence:

the frayed bridal train your chimneys lay
and the warped applause-track of Victorian rain.

You're the blackened lung whose depths I plumb,
the million windows and the smoke-occluded sun.

A girl steps from a door, her cotton flecked shawl
is the first snow on a turf-plot back in Mayo.

You're the globing of the world, a litany of little cities
cast and remade in your image: *Osaka, Orizaba, Gabrovo.*

Your warehouses bloated by curious needs:
butter, shellfish, clog blocks, bleach.

Your urchins little merchants hawking Lucifers and besoms
to set a small flame guttering in a wet-brick basement:

in the straw and wood shavings a mother's lullabies
bear their freight of love and typhus.

In the small hours I remake you and remake you,
until you grow faint as a footfall on a fever ward

and I wake from my imagination's gas-lit parlour
and whatever I seek to have or hold or harbour

is pure curio – a wreath of feathers, seashells
or human hair, a taxidermist's diorama.

Revenants

Tonight, as the kettle cools on the hob,
tour groups fold away their maps,
matching anoraks, stow walking poles,
forsake these lanes for the A roads,

their tyres hiss away like static on a radio,
there's a sense of something coming back;
outside the kitchen window the coffin path
emerges beneath the tourist track,

where dead generations were led
from godless towns to consecrated ground.
I see them, on a summer night struggling
with the big sling as if the body wrapped

within was simply dozing in a hammock,
the youngest bearer stifling a laugh
as if this was some May Day garden game.
Or at midnight when the winter rain

casts them in black and white,
like a moon-landing on a tiny TV screen:
I huddle in and watch a box fetched
clumsily across a harrowed field.

Such is the magnetism of the dead:
gypsies and suicides, consumptives and virgin brides
and the mother who bled to death in birth
all borne through snows and floods, over bridges

and stepping stones, across running water
the corpse's feet pointing away from home
to baffle the spirit from backtracking.
Such fear of haunting, such ritual in getting-rid,

they wobble like workmen carrying a fridge.
This is the pedestrian progress of the soul,
is rough-hewn homage and pilgrimage
travelling sun-wise, in straight lines.

Backlit by the silver the brook lobs up,
the corpse-candle of a luminescing barn owl,
carrying its cargo of light at ankle height,
pulling silence like a pall over the scene.

As we struggle through life:
shouldering our grief through the seasons,
names once on the tips of our tongues
now stones in our mouths.

But when we reach our journey's end:
No candle burns in the mother church.
No path beneath the crow's black mass.
No coffin-stone to rest the bones.

No witch ball hangs on the rowan tree.
Who'll walk the corpse road back to me?

Scar Tissue

When my hand finds your arm in the dark
more often than not, it's that glossy cicatrice
where one drunk winter you fell asleep
against the dull heat of a cast iron radiator.
My fingers map the known-world of its contour:
Your lonely archipelago, the keloid scar grows
and grows until it will not let either of us go.
Like a raised spade of earth at a burial,
the Greek *eschara*, your 'place of fire', defines you:

That intimacy with the impulses that drew
Joan of Arc to burn for love she could not name
and walking home in the drizzling rain
the man, inarticulate with rage, who flicks
a flame towards the shadow of the Cutty Sark.

The Leverets

That first winter, cooing around your pink face
at the cradle, the purr of the wood-burner
flicking its long tail out into the night sky.
I was sent to the car for nappies and formula
but froze when I saw it laid on the porch
the heavens condensed in its brown eye,
a frail bag of fur spilt a fine rope of gut
still warm to the touch as I went to move it.

Clawed from its nest into the cold world
sudden and bright and, in an instant, over.
This feline votive carried across neighbour's
fields with a safe breaker's swagger.
Then nothing, for years, until the birth of your sister.

Pallbearers

No stranger to crematoria
but still shocked so small
a casket could contain you,
your thirty thousand days,
a headland that slips clear
from view: your memories
of oceans, lovers, debtors,
the black cob you clicked
into a trot along a shingle
spit in childhood Norfolk.

We sat and wept, the raw
edge of a room's politesse:
neighbours, a night-nurse,
my grandmother a frail bird
on the lip of an open cage.
I thought of our last walk,
of processing under alders
little to share but comforted
by the other, of Neanderthal
skeletons covered in pollen,
of cataracts newly cut away
to admit, for one last time,
the light of all your yesterdays.

Silver Lake

'This life isn't all hookers-and-blow you know'
but even so one day a month you'd ease the car off
the boulevard, your u-turn describing a long slow arc
forgetting the pretence of work, the litter of scripts
on your passenger seat. Driving south
against the rush hour, the commute, as a salmon
might make its way, by force of will, upstream,
And so you headed out towards Tijuana.
I remember you saying you could order, as if from a menu.
How the oiled girls lined up to meet-n-greet you.
But I could not tell you which part of yourself you handed
over as your Buick crawled across the border.
Or which part of yourself you left forever
with Tanya, Tracy-Mae, Encarnacion or Estella.

COLM O'SHEA

Colm O'Shea was born in 1977 and grew up in Cork. He began writing poetry at school in between learning Irish grammar and doing sums. Realising that writing is a 'good way to keep dreaming when you're not allowed stay in bed', he has kept up the practice. He read English and Philosophy at University College Cork, then completed a doctorate at Trinity College Dublin. His PhD thesis (*Joyce's Mandala*) investigated *Finnegans Wake*, schizophrenia, and non-dual metaphysics. He recently completed a Masters of Studies in Creative Writing from Oxford University.

Prince of Frogs

Crrroak
I know what the princess dreams –
her pillow is slick with my toxins.
A golden ball,
just out of reach,
bounding slowly down a hill.

In the end it was not a kiss,
but the way I let her tantrum throw me,
excremental, against a wall,
that won her child's heart.
Such kind eyes, oh my prince!

Crrroak
Tonight I am a guest of the palace,
my pharmacy charming her dreamtoy
back down my well,
to be licked by an old flycatcher,
eyes slit with pleasure.

Too sultry to struggle now,
her mammal hairs are fever-twisted,
clumped with my secretions.
A swollen ball,
riddled with tadpoles,
a jellied mass – quivering.

Crrroak-crrroak-crrroak
Hear my brothers
calling in the mating night.
A golden bubble,
in the sucking murk,
swamped in a chorus of frogsong.

Corpse Pose

Death: Let all clichés soak into my skin,
tattooed to the moment,
perfumed to a heady synaesthesia,
and draped over a rusty country fence.

I've misplaced my skull –
set the eyeballs down somewhere
in the regional park
for some child to find
and use as soggy marbles.

I've pulled out my twitchless tongue
– long as a snake –
for a cat to munch on before feeling
the collywobbles

and hiding in the tall grass
to take a shit.
His cat-shame is almost unbearable
as he rounds his haunches,
snout quivering, glancing about.

My spine remains the Ballincollig stone wall,
curving back through my childhood
and crumbling into the future.

I left my hollow belly and bones
on a pub wall in the town;
tourist drinkers perceive
an archaeological exhibit –
an ancient set of uilleann pipes?

A dog stole my hands.

I've donated my genitals
to the vaudeville realm
where they can dance on the end of strings
as a marionette puppet
wearing specs and a false moustache –
a comic commentator on
the Great Striptease.

Bashō writes:
The temple bell stops
But the sound keeps coming
Out of the flowers.

But soaking through the ringing petals
ah! – such an easy silence
stretches along the park pathways,
arranging itself in the lines
of leaves on the ground
– glowing green and fading brown –
a tantalising history in cyphers
leading to the water's edge
where I enter the cool river,
not causing a ripple.

Night in the Workshop

Muttering to himself,
his hammered thumb still throbbing,
Daedalus fixes bovine skin
to a wooden-cow frame
as were the queen's orders.

Spending all that time
in the meadow,
with a white bull...
Kretan women are odd.

Asleep under starlight,
his sore thumb fashions
a wave of nightmare:
  Old Minos' millipede semen, squirming;
    endless convolutions
      through a dark, coiled habitat;
       an Attic exterminator
        creeping with red thread;
          the twisted horns of a cuckold's secret,
          stomping, furious, hidden beneath
         the base of a kingdom,
        gorged on a diet
      of innocents.

      Even the workman's regular dream
     – feathered flight! –
   is spoiled by
  obscure visions:
a mocking sea?

He wakes early
– recalling nothing –
and sets about finishing
Pasiphaë's commission,
his thumb recovered.

Such is the architecture
of the Labyrinth,
hammering itself into flesh.

Racing Atalanta

A husband will cause you to lose yourself,
yet you will not flee him.

OVID, Metamorphoses

1

Wanting a boy so badly,
Daddy doesn't notice his daughter is born
balanced on her two feet.
Next day, deserting her in the woods,
he just misses her first steps.
Artemis sent a bear to suckle her.
Untrue. Unhelped, the baby finds the bear,
forces herself to a teat.
Warm fur is better than lullaby –
she nestles amongst cubs.
It takes two stout hunters an hour
to haul her from the slaughtered sow
and claim the pelt.

2

Long-limbed Atalanta:
the stadium describes the circuit
of her immortality.
Spectator chants build, bleed into a howl:
the very wind cheers her. Her body is the best
of all poor substitutes for war –
a glorious animal display.
Her starting crouch is coiled victory,
all calf-curve, thigh tension, a low growl.
Jaded gods hush.
Her starter's mark is ten yards behind the men.
Thick-veined, muscle-knotted,
they glance back.
Their advantage is lost at the gun –
a blush of speed – she ravishes male pride,
pure as ice cracking its restraints.
The stars' stadium is cramped, a cage.

Packs circle as she jogs the streets,
baiting her when ignored: *Demon. Freak.*
Frigid monster bitch.
She shrugs.
I'll marry any man who overcomes me.

3

On quiet evening runs,
the ice-cream man abandons his van,
lumbering beside her for a few hundred yards.
Always this rushing.
Let me buy you a treat –
shoes without wings.
She nods no, trots on, but gift by gift,
each panted promise slows her, until,
succumbing to his bear hug,
she finds herself clinging
nightly tighter to his hairy chest
like life depends on it.
She strokes her stretching belly,
feels the kicks of her cubs,
sees the tiny victories she'll concede
racing them in the park, near the ducks.
Sundays are zoo days.
The lovers watch the lions yawn.
She sits to rest her back, and muses.
How swiftly anonymity comes.
He buys her a caramel apple –
bronze in the shade, gold in the sun.

Gingerbread

In a red winter dawn,
the pair panting through the forest
finally stop. They slump against a tree,
certain the bark stinks of burning flesh.

Still heaving,
Hansel's first thought is of bite-marks
in bread walls, linking them to the charred
corpse curled in the oven.

He regards his sister: holocaust-maker.
And home: what waits there?
A sturdy famine table,
the sunken cheeks of the starved-mad.

This cold soil smells scorched.
Hungry, he casts inedible jewels
deeper into the woods, make-believing
a trail. A dusting of snow sprinkles down –

ash, or powdered sugar.

SANDEEP PARMAR

Sandeep Parmar was born in Nottingham in 1979 and was raised in California. She received her PhD in English Literature from University College London in 2008. The subject of her research was the unpublished autobiographies of Mina Loy. She received an MA in Creative Writing from the University of East Anglia in 2003 and studied for her BA at the University of California, Los Angeles. She is reviews editor for *The Wolf* and is currently Member of High Table at Newnham College, Cambridge, where she is researching the writings of Jane Harrison and Hope Mirrlees. She is co-editing Mirrlees' *Collected Poems* for Fyfield Books (Carcanet) in 2011.

The Octagonal Tower

> *History is the love that enters us through death; its*
> *discipline is grief.*
> ANNE MICHAELS

I

Whatever rage has come through these sealed doors,
And scalded us black and frayed, we have no name for.
We cannot explain the quiet, sleepless shift of whispers,
A procession of shrouds along our corridors,

Or the diverted eyes that cloud to see a row of winter oaks outside
Shocked in their dendritic fizz. And if we do know it,
It is in the blood, in this terrible synapse of sky, in the road away.
From our house we drive down through a sunken valley
Where, like a crypt, it is forever the hour of the dead.

You have always worn the wheel, pushed your hands and wrists
Through its axes, as though it were a shackle. Driven, hunched.
It is the same – the sting of yucca and eucalyptus, a vein of pink
Bougainvillea purged in hot pulses off rooftops – a fragrant massacre –
And the same steady road you drive every time afraid to speak,
Afraid to ask when I will leave you alone in that house with your wife.
I translate your favorite song in my mind: *This song of mine, no one*
      will sing.
This song of mine that I sing myself will die tomorrow with me.

An October night, 1975. A sudden rain has liquefied the earth.
Mud isn't enough. There is a word you use that means more than mud,
It is the sound of a foot, sunken to the ankle, pulling itself out –
The awful suck of uprooting. Like a scream, it is the fear of standing
So long that you might stay and sink forever. This sound trails
Behind you and your brother as you walk the fields one last time.
You will leave and not return for ten years, to marry my mother
Who you've not yet met. Your four bare feet make an agreement with
      the earth
To remember. The earth prints its own response in your shadows.

II

Holidays are uncertain times. The marble face of an old king's grief
Deflects the spectacle of his queen's death in each perfect tessera.
The Taj rises above the Jammuna, doubles paradise in the mastery of
      slaves.

Holidays are uncertain times; their hands are cut off arms thrown up
In celebration. Now they too mourn, and skyward pray to phantom limbs
In the gardens of heaven, alone to pluck and preen.

They are carted away without ceremony, along with the remains of stone
that, like teeth, fall out of swooning heads. The funeral begins.
Mumtaz, hollow as a bride, is veiled in by her white, carved lid.

No one knows when you were born. They think it was an autumn month.
At five you asked where your mother was. Your false soot lashes pooled
    with fear.
Gone to your grandmother's. Later you found her picture.
A woman propped up, freshly dead, her hands emptied of the past.
And you, seated on her lap, two years old, holding her
And what held her forever in that exposure.

III

The road widens just past tracts of arched houses; you drive faster and
    grip the wheel.
I say I won't leave till after the New Year, but by now it doesn't matter.
Your knuckles are bloodless, and your stoic eyes are the calm surface of
    a timepiece.

Shah Jehan, imprisoned in a tower by his son, was sent a gold platter
The day of the coup with the head of his chosen heir upon it.
Seeing this the old king fell, knocked the teeth out of his head.
For eight years he watched the Taj from his window, from across the
    river,
In a diamond mounted in the wall that reflected it a million times over.
The soft marble hands of his wife extended to him, to the empty casket
    beside her.
When the river filled, he walked across it.

When the door opens, only one of us leaves. I watch your car until it is
    far down
Through the shadows of trees. The road receives you, and the house
    receives you,
As does the galley of water, the trimmed hedge, the cold, sterile cell.

In your wallet, you carry a picture of my mother, from before my birth,
When she was only yours. Her pinks match the pinks of flowers;
She bows her head into the branch and smiles, as beautiful as a queen.
Love is incidental, time-bound. Pain is eternal, is locked to it by memory.
It is the memory of love we love. It is the memory that fattens on pain –
Of these small deaths and these stone walls. The crown that has sunken
From your ears and hangs around your neck is all that remains.

Loy Returns to Paris

Le Bonheur   the bloodless mechanics of travel.
Kicking at space is no arrival.

You collect the child you left   now provincial
and round from planning menus, and improving her script
for four years in an Italian village.
Giulia's negrita Joella, her
curls browning illegitimately.

The rue Campagne-Premier,   a grey, hutched widow-latch
for a Poiret with fine bone structure.

Refurbished vanities choir on workshop tables.

Address books somersault, and a life is written
from 'Z' to pseudonym.

Curving fingers smelt graphite into cracks.   Fine noses
of inherited genius,
blackly spar and bring turtles
to your babies,   note their approving babble
for use in their trades.

Elbowed pages, snapped under books, crooked
deletions migrate   in the direction of an echo.
Festooned shadows bend over your youngest

Fa bene, dusting pillboxes, carrying coloured glass
from one childhood to the next.

Archive for a Daughter

November 1972, Derby

  A dance card embalmed in sweat.
       Her ruthless curve of palm
  mowing the carpet into sheaves before a gas fire.

Liquidescent virgin in a purple dress.
    Oil paint, shaded avocado, umbrella sun-wings.

Box 2, folder 20, 'Early Married Life'

a single page:
  recto
    a fashionable centre-parting
  verso
    consonants: midnight affair nuclear affair bleach affair
  watermark indecipherable

[But here we are jumping ahead]

The archivist notes that no exact birth date is known.
An already Western dressed 6-year-old reads the headlines
of English newspapers for party tricks.
Her black eyes are blunt and unequivocal like the prophecies of
    pharaohs.
In a Punjabi village, she and her impeccable mother, gemstoned,
    oracular,
princess a vernal causeway.

Box 1, folder 2, 'Emigration'

The BOAC stewardesses Max Factor crinkled baskets
of sweets to soothe the girl's swinging, impatient feet.
Aviation – a risky endeavour in 1963 – levels a curse at her progeny.
Aerophobia – her own daughter's –
fear of the air between home and exile collapsing.

Box 1, folder 7, 'Education'

Homelands Grammar School For Girls

Miss Moore leans across an oak sea and parquets a line of future mothers.
Her bovine sympathies, neatly pressed, tentacle
                              towards the only Indian in the class.
      The Georgian battlecross marking her forehead,
                              kindly and thoughtfully, segregates.

The girl bounds wildly through the Public Library –
Huxley to her 11-year-old mind suggests individuality –
            but the Savage's feet recommend no one specific exit.

   folders 8-17

Unbound Notebook, mostly unreadable:

*I thought I could become a doctor and asking found I could not think to ask
to become anything*

The archivist notes that these pages are not continuous.
Refer to Box 2, folder 10, 'Correspondence'.
A photograph of a prospective husband and several handwritten credentials.

Box 3, folder 1, 'Notes on Motherhood'

Nursery – pram – groceries – pram – doctor's visit –
                              cucumbers in half lengths –
– over each shoulder some conspicuous intellect –

Husband-academic, wife-typist
      She door-to-doors Hoovers, Avon, thick rosaries of factory lace,
while her children pop tic-tacs for invented ailments in plastic houses.

Nottingham hurls snowballs at her black turbaned gentleman.

      Soaked typescript, fair copy of a life –

When she asked her parents for a spare suitcase for an exodus,
      they replied, my child, *nothing is ever spare*

Box 4, folder 1, 'Exile'

1985, Vancouver – ablaze with cherry blossoms from here to the kindergarten.
We arrived with one steel pot, a bag of lentils and an onion.

folder 2

1987, North Hollywood – submarine fences root Thanksgiving potatoes,
one a piece. My daughter reads Laura Ingalls Wilder to her menagerie
of dolls. Raft sails calmly on.

folder 3

1989, Oxnard – Gifted children are pursestrings. We mind their collegiate
years with interest. El Rio wizens to a stockpile of citrus and rental agreements.

folder 4

1995, Ventura – Bibled to real estate, gold blazers cinch round a wade of
blonde, leathered adulterers. The neighbours tend their god-plots of lawn
and hedge.

Box 5, folder 1, 'Drs Parmar'

She saunas with the ladies of the Gold Coast –
　　one Japanese ex-comfort woman, one savvy señora
　　goldbuckled and multifranchised.

　　Stanford, Northwestern, Harvard, London, Cambridge –
　　and when my husband's sisters wept because I had no sons,
　　I said I have two doctors (one of body, the other of mind)
　　and sent my uterus via Federal Express to the village,
　　with my compliments!

On the verso, written in ink, is a page from Box 1, folder 8 [mis-
placed]

I remember clearly when I knew that I would one day die.
I was on the toilet and I was 11.
The bathroom was white and oblivious.

Chopin's Waltz No. 7

The Classics contrabanded in the cellar with rose petal jam.
(Rose petal Jam?) A week of breakfasts' invisible guest.
Husbands and fathers, too, ghosted every meal.
You were their substitute, rationed nephew, the favourite.

Feline cousins, Deanna and the other (what was her name?
Imagine Helen of Troy, only topless and more petulant)
each claimed an arm. Above ground, Tanti Ani boudoired
all day in a fuss with curlers and romance novels.

At dinner, she thumped the table and shouted, 'Rachmaninov!'
The stuffed peppers swallowed their tongues, the mish-mash
glistened indifferent. You rose, cigaretted, rolled your sleeves,
patterning clouds with your teeth into notes in the air.

Ani forgot her communist meanness, her housedress, her wigged
ugliness. (Where had her husband gone?) Partnered alone
to Chopin's No. 7 (*Walzen* is to roll, revolve, to shove blame),
she debutanted like a Hapsburg princess in a scandaled room.

Tempo cut slow enough to let the mind finger its black stakes
back, mindful not to displace the past, the relics of conspiracies,
black lists, shots to the temple. She could have hung herself
and swayed, smiling for you who never wanted to leave.

Recuerdelo

(for Parveen)

Your word comes back
a caution not to act   after the act

Picking blackberries in Leah's yard
away from her mother
who had locked herself   in the bathroom

We were young   and bled easily into incautious hands
the thin-skinned spoils of weeds

In every month there were roses
given women's names
dried in Santa Anas by day   to be laid heavy with dew
at night when they dream   of floating
on seamless lakes   with hands at each sloped bank
that tremble and reach
but cannot break their sleepless sleep

Your word blinks away an ocean through an invisible porthole
It is how we remind ourselves   what does it mean

That secret tongue   impermissible as poverty
the smell of mixed fats frying
of lumbered bellies and their shirts   rising

The eager hands   inching up simple and sudden and silent
like the raising   of a dawn-lit window

HEATHER PHILLIPSON

Heather Phillipson was born in 1978 and brought up in London and Wales. Her poems have been published in magazines and commissioned by the BFI. She was awarded the Michael Donaghy Poetry Prize from Birkbeck College in 2007, and won an Eric Gregory Award and a commendation in the Troubadour Poetry Prize in 2008. Her Faber New Poets pamphlet is published in October 2009. Alongside her poetry, Heather is also an artist and exhibits nationally and internationally, and won the Sir Leslie Young Artist Award in 2009. Recent exhibitions include Bloomberg New Contemporaries 2008 and 'Formal Incidents', a solo show in London in 2009. She was Artist in Residence at London College of Fashion in 2008-09, and works as a freelance exhibition reviewer for a-n magazine.

Ablutions

The bathtub makes me weak –
my heartbeat under water.
Salts, oils, sodium laureth sulphate;
listless moisture laps my slopes:
I am a mountain in a lake.
From the corridor, *The Romantic Sounds of Xavier Cugat.*
I synchronise my loofah.

My big toe turns the hot tap.
Oh God, the changing temperature of bathwater!
Hot and cold I understand;
tepid means less than ever.
How hard it is to get things right.
How devastating you looked today across Soho Square
in your pink cashmere sweater,
your man bag over your left shoulder.
Like soap I am loquacious
and I give myself up trying to say it.
Who was it that first thought of washing?
Your eyes are blue, I have loved you
since I noted your lashes in profile.
I didn't do it deliberately –
I was distracted
the way foam is distracted from water
and clings all over my contours.

Crossing the Col d'Aubisque

I could say a lot about a lot of things, but my heart
knocks at the bends, or at you in profile,
and I'd rather hear the stereo. We're right on the edge
of the roadway, the clouds, and of knowing each other,
and sometimes The Smiths are in synch
with what I don't express: driving, familiarity,
the line between intimacy and dying.
Our breath's on the windscreen.
I've left my shoes in the boot.

I want to call out to the horses in the mist:
I've known so much about insignificant things.
I've known nothing. Not like the way a horse
knows grass. I count all the men I've ever kissed.
But I'm with you; I'm almost over the verge,
and, if we slid off now, the privilege would be mine –
not to know if it was the beginning,

or the end, or your bad steering,
or my fault for, say, at that moment

reclining my seat. I'd know my red toenails
against your walnut-trim dashboard
and I'd cry out to the horses:
'It wasn't the hairpin bends; it was something else!'
I'd know you in ways
they can't understand: high up, brief.
Let me change gear while you drink pear juice.
Beyond your bonnet is the rest of the world.
Mountains – I can barely see them.

Devoted, Hopelessly

The only men it's safe for me to love are dead –
O'Hara, Stevens, Berryman.
They send me to my desk, or off to Hackney Central –
to get black grapes, fit, and ideas.
Simon's hair was black and untameable.
Tuesdays, I stop at the library for poetry.
Hair's all very well; ideas take commitment.

At twenty-eight Charlotte Brontë feared herself a spinster.
Married soon after; died in pregnancy. I make marginalia:
'women are getting older all the time' etcetera.

Sam wrote 'Marry me!' in the snow outside my window;
his cheese on toast was persuasive, but a distraction.
Days pass with such things.
I didn't hold his hand tightly enough. He left me
a message: 'We all need to be editors.'

I eat grapes from the bag, unwashed,
read the Index of First Lines aloud,
and tell myself 'I need to be alone to be more'.
I meet Ben, by chance, by the derelict jobcentre.
He tells me: 'There's a lot of bad love going around.'

Make a note, check the pavement. On the ground
a snail's a comma or an apostrophe, dependent on context.
I will rescue it from the footsteps of pedestrians
with their pedicures and lace-ups and love
of romantic fiction and coffee in cardboard cups,
take it on a detour down a side road.

German Phenomenology Makes Me Want to Strip and Run through North London

Page seven – I've had enough of *Being and Time*
and of clothing. Many streakers seek quieter locations
and Marlborough Road's unreasonably quiet tonight,
and humid. If it were winter I'd be intellectual, but it's Tuesday
and I'd rather be outside, naked, than learned –
rather lap the tarmac escarpment of Archway Roundabout
wearing only a rucksack. It may be useful
for reduced ciabatta from the 24-hour supermarket.
I can't read any more of Heidegger's *Dasein*-diction,
I say as I kick off my slippers.

When I speak of my ambition
it is not to be a Doctor of Letters
or to marry Friedrich Nietzsche, it turns out,
or to think better.
It is to give up this fashion for dressing.
It is to drop my robe on the communal stairs
and open the front door onto the commuter hour,
my neighbour, his Labrador, and say nothing
of what I know or do not know, except what my body says.

James Grieve

Golden-cheeked, it glided in above a scarf
of the kind worn by men who play chess:
I saw your apple before I saw your face.
And marvellous how you could make it last
strategically, it seemed, by eating less
and talking more, as though each bit that passed
your lips were a course in some slow repast;
your restraint! I was ravenous, riveted to my place.

My Braeburn I bite at eight o'clock; you lovely thing,
you made me do it. The window suspends
the creases of the evening sky, my clothes fold to the floor
like hot towels. Vivid as the crimson curtains, I sing
canticles from the second storey as if all flesh depends
on the sinking of teeth through air: premise of our rapport.

You're an Architect and I Want to Make Dinner for You

Just as I slice the treacle tart you halt my hand,
ask me to regard its lattice. You elaborate with permanent ink,
kitchen paper – your ideas sink through to the table. Steadily,
evening arrives from the East.

My bedsit is modest, my world is changing – seated
opposite you and your 0.2 fineliner, it includes all possible
universes. The pastry is homemade. We dream in multiple
        dimensions –
lines are trellises, extensions, non-Euclidean geometries –
see, you say, how the shortcrust lets us see beyond it! Yes,
our windows will be curvilinear. I pour the cream,
neatly fold your drawing (twice), nearly forget to eat.

Taking Breakfast Alone

Halfway through a soft-boiled egg,
half-full of tea, I'm in need of something sweet.
If you were here you could pass me a Digestive, darling,
feed the cats and me. Every day
I might come close to death and not know it
and so I go on eating without urgency
and releasing crumbs like rainfall on my sheets,
as if time won't come to an end here while you're away.

But I might drown in bed and biscuits
in the height and heat of the day.
I might slip as I run to answer the doorbell
and it'll be the postman's fault I'm not quite fulfilled, waiting
for your postcard, or Samuel Beckett from an internet bookseller.
Maybe I'll lie back in the crumbs like a river
and let them find their level around me, just as you
lounge on sand somewhere, I suppose, and listen to the sea.

Or are you downstairs?
I hear you slicing toast and cursing.
But you are way up in Denver.
I am deranged with sugar.
Men are cutting up the road outside my window, swearing at the sun.

KATE POTTS

Kate Potts was born in 1978 and grew up in South London. She worked in Music Publishing before studying Creative and Life Writing at Goldsmiths' College, London, then trained as a teacher at the Institute of Education. Kate has taught English and Creative Writing in Further and Adult Education Colleges in London for several years, and has also worked on reminiscence projects with older people suffering from dementia. In 2006 she was overall winner in a Booktrust Creative Writing Prize for teachers, and her poetry was commended by New Writing Ventures in the same year. Her first pamphlet, *Whichever Music*, was published by tall-lighthouse in their Pilot series in 2008. A Poetry Book Society Pamphlet Choice, it was also shortlisted for the first Michael Marks Award for Poetry Pamphlets.

Galatea / *Pygmalion*, Sunday morning

Ignite at the eye's cool centre, haul the onioned iris
wider – wormhole gnawing at blue – tight witness.

Avoid the look of the eyes – pale meat –
grit oysters – spit-swabbed.

Your mind clump's February's pudding, hinged
like tinny umbilical, milk-tooth, twisting. Worry it.

There's a hint – peat gone-ness of intestine
but she's cauterised, more stone than skin.

Worry the names: mattress warp, soft eel of stunned
body – hot consonants radioed in to new maps.

She'll outlast you – modelled as if set to spring,
twitching now – vigilant temples, lashes –

Broadcast the nerve. Branch current through
methylate tissue. Hang to the ion, pulse,

though mimicking litheness can be
puppetry – seized string –

shake smoke, draggle sleep –
scoop the cuttered, yellow-tree morning

and drink the exposure, the flush
configuration –   his features, face.

Flit

Like a Wednesday matinee film, this leaving, a last
slow burn and a skip out, his sly mouth drawn thin.
Your new-cooled eyes survey the walls, the plaster
fractures, blue dust laid in pelts. You're loose,

skinned – a stark brew – prodding the bag of leaves
as if it holds last tannin, last tea-kick – strong
as a horse – husked chords on the phone to the office.
You're not yourself. You're someone ductile, burnished.

You – thick-lipsticked, filling a canvas bag with apples,
the end of a loaf. The chemist hawks lotion, sunglasses,
bleach. You – minnowing up the baked streets,
sharper, each tread slicing August clean open. You –

sleek purpose, stalled on the station concourse,
mouthing the litany of departures, prising the coast
and spitting the rest of the fruit. Then headed out,
hitched to the engine's momentum, lighter

as the land falls. You – picture postcard – skirting
the main street, kicking at dune-shins, wallowing further,
treading water. The cowl of your new-shed skin's
a cool star, a map point away on the shingle,

cupped in the tideline's tar and trash. You – hours on –
salted, dried, and sewn back in, hugging the hook
of your knees, gums a swill of vinegared chips and wine –
the pip and blurt of the arcades hauling you in, slowing,

loping back to the town's eyes, train's cradle.
Concourse. Clay city-streets. Stupefied bed.

Proof, Maybe

The light's buttercups – quick, mossed water.
Mister, behind the lens layer, scopes her:
grand, fly-goggle glasses and cribbed grin,
dog lead slung loose around her neck.

We daughters – her ducks – putter behind,
lagging, diminishing in height.
We girls, armed with buckets, shrimp-nets,
and our own, more brittle cameras.

His one, gigantic eye dilates, tightens –
pure cornea – calculated focus and aperture,
a question of degrees.

We took the girls out to Westerham. It was August.
Swish car, upholstery, house in the city,
a dopping of learning about your name – *Doctor* –
remember that phone book call in the early hours,
the man whose wife was giving birth?

We are squinting in gingham, growing, intractable.
Not insomnia's spite, cussed day, kicked teeth
but an accumulation of glossy paper,
irrefutable fact, brisk walks.

Kafka had a sign over his desk that read, simply, WAIT.
Words seize – bleach – are not enough.

Sedna

That day of dog heat we
scanned timetables then slung our bodies coastward,
wheat stubble, scrublands and
redbrick all blown sheer to honeyglass, bowed
in the engine's slipstream and us –
rocketing back to the big salt, like lost amoebae.

Schlepping thin, membrane soles
over gravel and rock-silt to the water I did not
tell you I'd seen the ocean floor,
that raw soup's pillowing slip and heave, gravity
snowing me in, a uterine wad
of sea, strands setting like plum liquor.

I only coddled the cold, malachite pip
lodged, bitter in my belly, lobbed
slicks of ripe weeds, felled you by your
skinny ankles, tombed toes in the
wet sand, numbed the bitter
hook of that seed with iced lager.

Compendium of Water

○ Roof-leak, drench for beached fins, first and last thing –
  branded, filched glassfuls.

○ Litre jugs drunk pig-cheeked, barefoot, poured
  and lain in, pruning skin to mush, feet to webbing slaps.

○ Chiming pints, bedside and bath edge, crusted,
  condensing, sweet as ulcer and gum.

○ Possibility nurtured by hills, that last scarp,
  premonition of slug's trail sea.

○ Pipes bark, trundle –
  the whale-cry of solitary, braking buses.

○ Insomnia chant for a child slipping, flat-footed,
  as if over snow, down to the kitchen's lowing, sink –

○ this hankered spool of light, transmuted, tap to tongue.

Misapprehensions

When I was a child I spake as a child, I understood as a child...

A dog, fed chicken bones, will swell,
sore like an ulcered gum. Red hives
will pucker and inflate, each a sticky itch.

Though rabbits are gluttons, lawns
belong to us all: their casual lips bless knees.
There's a ghost in the bathroom, skulking

between the lines of the black-tiled wall,
watching me brush my teeth. It all depends
on his temper, the hollow breathing of pipes,

their temperamental shudder. Tap the ceramic
and he hides. Tread carefully. Don't tread.
Don't tread on the paving's edge. BLAM –

a blossoming flash – magnesium white –
the greasy wires of shopping trolleys
are twisted guts of unfortunates.

Magic keeps us alive, but all food poisons us,
slowly. Stairs are a monument, the mud-clod edge
of the cliff that crumples under your heel

as you plummet asleep
to rest in god's giant, marble palm:
unfurling, trusting, blind.

Greyhound to Syracuse

Pig-dog, huddle of cottons and belly,
he's flung unconscious. I see
wood-panel homesteads, shacks,
abundance of pine, pine, pine;

the woodlands smear green past.
I snout the window glass. He sought
me out. At Buffalo, in line, I was the spit
of this actress, that Heather, Callisto –

whatever – my sleep-creases
and darkling eyes, waning, heavy
lidded, my skinny wrists. He's bussed
for five days solid, headed for a state

with better Medicaid. We worked
his English accent up. The vowels
quivering, filmy – for his Lennon
turn, his tricks, my approbation.

He slugged his pills with Gator pop.
I crushed a cheek to the glass
to gawp at land, skid to knock-out
night, to your apparition, love –

CGI in this shunt of jump cuts.
You have no scent. My hands
whip through, knuckles
stuttering on in strobe light,

your wheel-beat scintilla no foil
for matter – nerve, nor skin.
We pull in for a border security team.
The cops chitter thinking they've got one –

they're mistaken, so we drive on,
gone sleep-sour, our hands
chilled. At Syracuse, he shakes
my little finger as he goes.

SOPHIE ROBINSON

Sophie Robinson was born in 1985. She has a BA in English Literature and an MA in Poetic Practice. Her poetry often deals with the complicated relationship between technology, culture and the female body. She is currently undertaking a practice-based PhD in queer poetics and existential phenomenology at Royal Holloway, University of London. Her work has been included in *The Reality Street Book of Sonnets*, and her chapbook, *a*, was published by Les Figues Press in 2009. She currently lives and works in London.

Geometry No. 1
(for Aerin Davidson)

The upright nature of a girl, belied by
formless whirrs, signs of visible lust like the
density of skies, & the disappearing hour;
I think of you urgent & weak walking beside
billboards, missing out, flaking off in the
silence between 2 traxx, no tender riot
in yr geekheart [spliced open & pulsating
in four different places whilst the summer

is blaring musty and lithe, awful shiny
skin & sick tune of birds germinating light
as a new kind of loudness] & the crude urban
cosmos misses you & is just passing the
time w/dirt & money & pouting in the
corner w/out your nocturno-suspicious lure.

Geometry No. 4
(for Aerin Davidson)

This our night, hands clasped on the last instant it
saw to the skirt, jump up & clap in a
second, their eyes met over the pond in
that lean death of words, that stagnant
lang of stirring, that ground glitch or near
touch that gleams & scarce makes contact before
singing in the wind away from 'how pretty
you are' & all that blood that dances so,
& now we all have our own rooms to not
touch in, little slips of things w/vomit
to spew on cushions & my bed is mine
alone & yes didn't the cautiousness
of human gesture surprise you? We cannot
do it anymore, our own hearts exceed us.

Disorder
(for Aerin Davidson & after Francesca Woodman)

our olfactory bed REPRESENTATIVE
OF a century of the self defiled
& nearly on the same page as me,
an influx of stallions & air around
you like an amputee [AIR is the language
that disappears] o this crashing intens
ity *a dichotomy of moving*

141

alone in this place this place a tiny
lobe of history & masochistic
switchblades plastic sockets made for my
fingertips my fingertips are coding|
the measurements of the sun & of loss
w/ the taste of flowers in my throat &
a large-scale projection of the female
form against my own who screams she screams w/
disease & time & nothingness murderous
reverberations placed w/in a system
by hero of software-for-itself whilst
babies & insects left alone will cry
& we harness samples of smudge & ghost
& exposure will kill us all in shutters
OR starry starry nausea as a
Manifestation of potential desires
We can't afford & all the memories
Wired into your knees lift you from the ground
Full of plastic-bag spirit & the promise
Of coffee & it's so cruel to never be

There always walking half out of shot.

unspeakable

Your name swallows my lips &
the backward downward rage of all
girls knocking through me, a risk of
speech a risk of love a risk of causing
a scene, zipper of my jeans against
yours & in your ear I hear the sea.

Your name reverses itself on my lips as
I swallow the anger like a little boy, a
battle of the body, a risk of method, the
receipt of love, the cold slither of a fence
against the zipper of my jeans & the
immediacy of your ear against my face.

Your name; the danger of inversion,
swallowing down everyone's rage you
burn & shake beyond yourself you
are the danger of love & you press
your ear against the zipper of my
jeans & say 'I can hear the sea'.

Your name & mine.
Swallow it down.
We invert girls we slither under
barriers we shock with proximity
we press our ears to the ground
in search of foreign pleasures.

Your name & mine, swallowed
downward in anger. The reversal
of the body, scars where the
danger of love obtained will show,
our fingers in our ears our
hands pressed against our eyes.

ac/dc lover

clinging on by a singular prefix,
luminary engineering looms large
over flea markets of imagination
coursing voltage, hi speed peep
geeks engaged in crosstalking,
bleed process slowing against
the barrier of artefacts or the
freak economy which stroking
your delicate face has razored
edges threatening to push your
dissed head under nose filling
chlorine stenched streak of loss,
betamax tears streaming down
loads your torso, mode flit un

steady & sweating pixels in
space of tactical precision made
messy w/optical concerns,
quelle-o-matic squeals breaking
the ice cracks in a capable system
a lyric superwrap conjuring
difference split sharp hairpin
aching like a professional pinstripe
& setting the radio on fire every
leg has a part of play foot inching
to boom central love or idea of
it in viewfinder barely in the room
for federal media men down sinks
poured away faxed or blowdried out
at 300 vaults lower lip pinch firm
back on giggling cupped cold wall
of a hobbyist's wet struggle,
stroking the suit-quote quietude
mechanically – sick looks breathless
looks – adapt to shiver, grin sizzle
or ache in filter format, wet-hot
inside the sun's district, pumping
coercivity as far as it will give –
industrial silicone smirk sending
kisses to herself, honey-muscled
& passionately bare with use, buck
down on the detour & burst open
all over the table, oxidate-me-quik I
am a sensation-bound toy, a fiddling
timeshare a silky purchase zip in the
stitch of her digital entrance a fervent
fax unscrewed all over your throat.

duet in darkness

1 – violent pulpy mass, pale and silvery lines
of normal life fading, the suggestive world
in postwar thirst-o-rama thrall or sting of
eyes against spine, surround me then – mark me
badly on the supraorbital bed –

2 –   far from
     the passive transparency of parasites
subacute feelers groping in my abdomen,
a bitter turn or sensation with several
points of pressure, I shall pamper your numbness
with extending motions of my greasy jaundiced
chest, damp heaviness of discourse weighing up
our universal meat which glints in flashlight
amelioration, weeping dialectically.

1 – & encircling our implicated impairments,
which we covet, our heritage of lovecraft's
abstract ideals on the mantle like a wornout
star – gas & dust making us nauseous in our
excess & I long to syringe the disturbed
whites of your eyes with sugarwater, honey
running from your nose in excitement you
turn to me & vomit in a practical way,
tired of running in this trembling weather,
tongue ulcerated, rough as a cathedral wall...

2 –   emotionally erect, my night-eyes are
exhausted, moans seep through in auditory
fullness, you prostrate on the grass, covered in
ants & stiff with cervical grief, a bright-yellow
coldness clinging to everything vertical in
lieu of anything happening.

we too are drifting

our tenderness being muttered up by other
people I lie awake twisting & stripped
of physical dwelling; hips with the same
feeling finding myself mumbling 'I'm sorry
we jerked' & your mouth is a place to go
a place where the human need for (relative)
peaceful sanctuary can collect itself –
suck me – nuzzle me – foster me – we are
in our separate spaces mouths mouthing
along to the words of the film *Patch Adams*
& learning that returning to "home" as an
adult promotes restlessness; but let's keep
kissing & dipping with friction against
the softness of *'Hum Sweat Hum'*, licking punk
I found myself dwelling in the conceptual
heart of nonsense breaking up, I have two
hands to cope with this death by values by
economix, we are locked in structure in
spite of our nylon surgings, them being
reduced to slits of marginal import &
we know better huh, & yes you the
eternal optimist you turn to me & say
that it's good to get perspective on a
perspective even when the sky's so black
with clouds it looks like night (upon which
you would remark at least that we are less
visible under extreme conditions &
besides we have more fun after dark)

synthesis

Unavailable little cuts on your scalp
or breath like sour dough, sharp little
teeth & you take me by the hand & run my
lips against your torso your torso an icy
statue, unavailable like little cuts on your shins the price of
being a woman, if that's what you are.

You blow your sour breath over the alien little
Crosses on my scalp, your small teeth pointed & I long
To kiss you. You take me by the hand & run
My lips against the image of your breasts;
Little crosses that are cuts that are the
Price of being a woman, if that's what you are.

Your box your mouth taste of vodka
against mine, skin all leather as we
lie against ourselves & maybe we
could peel it over & start. Sharpness
spreads & envelops us cuts our
breasts it is the price of being.

Untransferrable little crosses on your scalp your
saliva an acid paste my blood full of clots full
of the price of being a woman, if that's
what I am. You run my lips against your
box & the series of small cuts on your
shins which spell something out.

You are drunk & we breathe
into each others' mouths, the impact
of your skin is irreversible.
Your armpit, our lack
of proper tools, all these
small failures, the sharp price of being.

JACK UNDERWOOD

Jack Underwood was born in Norwich in 1984. He graduated from Norwich School of Art and Design in 2005 and is currently studying towards a PhD in Creative Writing at Goldsmiths' College, where he also teaches English Literature. He is a librettist, musician and co-edits the anthology series *Stop/Sharpening/Your/Knives*. He won an Eric Gregory Award in 2007, and his Faber New Poets pamphlet is published in October 2009. He lives in Hackney.

Toad

Toad, I have told you already,
this is not your house. Why do you insist
on staying there under the sink?
You cannot eat the soap like that,
it makes your insides sick.

I remember toad, the shed we used to sit in.
How, in the fizzing light of a twenty-watt bulb
you were moved to unbutton love, to turn
your pockets out and inspect the lint and sand
in the oil palm of your toad hand.
You were friendly in the sawdust then,
your toad face wide as the brim of your hat.

You cannot eat the soap like that.
Toad, it makes my insides sick.

Weasel

So Weasel, it has come to this;
to your thighs like tall glasses of milk,
your biscuit hair,
eyes that are like any kind of deep water.
It has come to those coiled, snaking guts
we had when we were younger still –
those balled-up sock guts of an afternoon
stolen back from college.
It has come to the spastic, ticking urges
rising through skin at the simplest
repositioning of your weasel hips,
or the one in twenty-seven kisses
I might land about your mouth,
of the right temperature and diction.

Was I even hungry once for eating?
Were you ever not the end to all fasts?

Your horse

has arrived and is bending himself into the room,
refolding his legs. I knuckle his nose,
which reminds me of the arm of a chair.

He is talking low and steady,
rolling back an eye towards his chestnut brain.
Man-words are climbing his long throat.

I show him to the bathroom
and he is embarrassed. Next he is hoofing
through your photo album.

There are more of me than of him.
We are crunching on polo mints together
and remembering the way your body used to move.

Wilderbeast

In the wilderness the devil came to me,
big antique horns, a swinging red dick
and my father's angry voice.

He offered me grapes, a puckered teat
loose with wine and milk. I spat.
And he spat back, my mother's maiden name.

I pressed on, urged my feet. Satan changed tack;
swam me in sensation: my first time drunk,
the heat of a well spun lie, boyhood

glimpsed between a hairdresser's breasts,
the smell of shampoo and cigarette breath.
Then from a tuck in his arse he pulled rain,

and a chip shop queue, the taste of shandy,
wet football boots dangled by the laces,
acorns and conkers tumbling from their spouts.

I gave a shout, a kind of grief escaping
and from astride his chin appeared
two slim girl's legs, akimbo his beard.

He opened his ripe mouth, folded his tongue back
and in, wriggling pleasure from himself,
stamping it out on the bare earth, braying.

I felt hunger folding in my gut.
The devil swung his hips, each jerk giving birth
to a pair of round, pert tits. *I am a good man!*

I railed, and each flesh sack withered and slapped
on the ground, sizzled on the grit-heat of rock.
I heard waves, an ocean then. But it was Satan

shushing with a four-knuckled finger to his lips.
A breeze faltered and caught over, sea birds swung
in long arcs. The devil leaned in and touched me,

150

quietly, here and then here.
Softly he drew a perfect circle on the ground
bid me dream my mortal desire inside it.

I took out a photograph of you my love.
Showed him grace: fixed and flattened,
wrapped in a scarf and coat last week,

when the camera pinned you to the sea
and I watched it happen from behind the lens;
my breath holding you there a moment.

I showed the devil your photo and he wept.
Flies fell buzzing from his cheeks.
You tempted and turned him

and the sun strained to look,
as the perfect circle became a pool of water,
hardened into a mirror,

the mirror I've been staring into since,
in our bathroom, in our flat,
with the wilderness of seconds between us.

Bonnie 'Prince' Billy

He is also singing how I will split
the atom and leave it for you cleaved
in two on the breadboard like an apple,
will peel your star-sign off the sky,
dissolve and serve it hot in a cup.

He sings how ugly and complex
I have become, sitting at the table,
gripping the stupidity of wood.

He sings how deeply I am weakened
by a single drip of water
falling from the end of your nose
and soaking into my jeans
like an excuse into the wider scheme of things.

Taking Back

Wasn't it great to feed old Tabitha,
the eating plant? Stunning the bugs
with a fizzing blue light, fobbing them down
the fun-pipe of our hungry hungry-queen.

Next day there was never any sign,
no wing-clot or stray leg in sight,
not even scorch marks on the bulb;
old Tabitha had licked the whole room clean.

We had to move out, so chucked her in a skip.
What's left of those nights lifts a leaf or leg
beneath the fudge of old bins.

I imagine finding her again, jaws open,
aghast. But that's the trouble with the past;
you can never take back the things you put in.

Maths

To commemorate the grand bazaar
the king is given a prize goat (x)
that is one and a half metres high.
Given that a prize goat eats
ten square yards of grass a day,
how long should the leash (y)
be tied so the prize goat can roam free
and feed until the next bazaar?

To the man who can give an answer
in yards and show his working,
goes the talcum hand of the virgin princess
who is also one and a half metres high.

Men come. One brings a ball of string
and a cauliflower to show he is both wise
and humble, another swings a bag of seeds,
two brothers flex their matching red braces.

So the suitors measure, scribble, compare
their feats of mind, strength
and faith. Bunting feathers the eaves,
a local man juggles numbers through the streets
dressed in the fleece and horns of a buck.
The princess bites her lip, her hair plaited
with ribbons the colours of her country.
Meanwhile the goat goes hungry.

Pelican

I stood in the shade of Pixie's beehive,
in the queue for a downtown movie theatre.
They were showing *Buzzsaw Zombies V*

for the third week running
and I was quickly falling in love.
'We can do it right now in the ladies' room'

I said. 'I'll stand inside this grocery bag.
If they hear noises and check under the door,
they won't be able to see my feet.'

That was the first time we spoke. The final time
I'd had the engine put back in my car
and wanted to take her with me.

She was standing outside the big Aquarium
and her dress had a round blue 1950s fish on it.
I shouted over 'Pixie, I love you.

I bought you some sunglasses.
My aunt has a cabin up in Pennsylvania
and I want you to live with me!'

But she just shoved me the finger and flashed
the pink sequined heart
on the front of her perfect knickers.

My hands went sticky and I cried all the way
to the interstate. Her sweetness had turned my heart
to cookies. I could feel the sun sinking

in my stomach. Driving past the forecourt
of a roadside diner, a fifteen-foot plastic pelican
looked very very sad.

AHREN WARNER

Ahren Warner was born in 1986 in Oxford and grew up in Lincolnshire. He has lived in London for the past four years and is currently working on a PhD at the University of London. He has published poems, and the occasional review, in various magazines including *Poetry Review* and *The Wolf*, as well as in the 2008 Tower Poetry anthology. Ahren recently received an Arts Council England Writers' Award to facilitate his work towards a first collection. His first pamphlet is due from Donut in 2010, with a book-length collection to follow from Bloodaxe a year later. He co-organised New Blood, a monthly night for young poets at the Poetry's Society's café in Covent Garden from 2006 to 2008. His other interests include visual art and art theory, pre-Socratic and post-Heideggerian ontology and aesthetics, Happy Hardcore and early 90s Gabba.

la brisure

each toll sustains itself   as if expecting
its own next sounding   or   another's

to which it will defer   by default   falling
to its own lack   its spacing from the other

each space comes   tactile   as a relief
or   as the rough joint-lines of a bronze

the repetition   of a hollowed   motif
the becoming sound   of the bronze

so each bell seems   to long
for an end   less partition   than party

a silence on which   each sound hangs
for its self-sameness   its being *partie*

you listen   to the last toll   draining
retained only   in the space   it becomes

you're unsure   if you're still waiting
or hearing   what has come

'discourse amounts to a disclosing of existence' *

As the hoplites sobbed *Thalatta!* to the sea
and we read of them in Xenophon, or *Ulysses*,
but felt nothing

        or if not nothing, not that silt
of earth and sweat giving to tears, then rivulets
which, reaching the lips, would taste half of dirt
half of the sea

so, I can't stop thinking of you,
Elisabet, or the arc you make of yourself
beneath

the pressure of two palms around the stretch
between your navel and your breasts, and careless
beyond the etiquette of *noli me tangere*

and though I know
such words come closest but always end up shadows
or tangles of analogue static

too worn to hear
the subtle tightening of the diaphragm
to which we all aspire

come here, if you want;
prove me wrong and (if Heidegger is to be believed)
show me your *Dasein*; I'll try to show you mine.

* Martin Heidegger: *Being and Time*

Beach
(after C.K. Williams)

The sea-breeze is cold and his words contract
the small, interior conglomerate of muscles
men of faith might call the soul.

He ambulates fear so delicately, those human tones
of despair. I do not know if it's the spray of salt
buffeting my lips that is the cold.

Inside, you let the spray course through your hair
the water rolls down your back, narrows its path
through the nook of your spine, falls at and around your toes.

I snag my breath on the rush of air, the depth
of misery he conjures in a few uncommon words
though we see it every day:

a jaw tensed like a scaffold, the twitch of skin
ill at ease on its frame, smiles that seem pleas.
I slow lick the sea from my lips and turn

to our room where you sit. I want to lick
the water that beads to your skin
the soft relief of something that fits.

'About suffering they were never wrong, The Old Masters'

Though, when it comes to breasts, it's a different story.
Cranach, for example, never seems to have progressed
beyond his pubescent attempts at apprenticeship;

tennis balls sewn to a pillow of hay, fingers coming
to terms with the concept of foreplay. So too
with Titian, whose Venus bares handleless plungers

or the fruits of a template mocked up at Bellini's.
For breasts, you want Rochegrosse, his *Chevalier*
surrounded by breasts real enough to have men

gripping their gallery plans discreetly; or Picabia
at his most garish: his naked, peroxidised blonde
stretching to coddle her slavering mutt. Her breasts

impress their tender weight upon us, and though
not as lofty as Pieter would have liked, she too
knows something of our weakness; that we fall,

or are floored, as much by the salt lure of skin.

Aristotle is a ____

'I'm in love with detail. Chestnut trees'
SEAN O'BRIEN, 'Walking'

Not the vagaries   of sprawled   variegated leaves
or the monotony   of rows of tree after tree
but this canyoned   ridged   knot   half dying wood   half moss

that   makes its cranny at the foot   of a burnt-out stump
and if sketched   would be feigned   with approximate lines
by an eye   unqualified to deal in minutiae.

Yet   such detail is here;   the cragged bark   petrol seared
the odd ribbed louse   the intestinal villi of moss
the etched insignia: *kezza n' nosh woz ere.*

This last one is our *ex machina*   a middle finger
to black lines on white pages   to the sanitised sign.
Bow down   to this make-shift god   of pen-knife and passion

like kezza   at nosh's request   moving to genuflect.

159

I *La Carte Postale*

As we say arboretum   here   I walk below the *arbres*
down the Rue Jussieu   amongst the mottled *ombre*.

The books shrink on their stalls   the shop walls crack
to craquelure.   The Seine might be the Acheron

if Eliot had got his langue on.   The *cafés* brim.
The heat   ensures an ambery slick   above the upper lip

part pimento   tar   and garlic   but miscible
with the Beaujolais   I'm drinking by the bottle.

From bed   I hear Emmanuel   the bourdon
bell   (At Notre Dame   the tourists shout him down.)

Outside   the traffic drones   a Pérotin melisma.
As always   I think of you   I wish that you were here.

II *K.304 (Tempo di Menuetto)*

The books shrink on their stalls, the shop walls crack,
panes begin to stutter,

the pigeons take their leave, foundations shudder;
shuck their own six feet of earth.

The rubble forms – a rough cartography of our fall –
dust flukes upon the air.

Here, I hold your tongue, its ferric tang, the way
it sets the moon beyond the body.

III *Works and Days*

As rubble forms   its rough cartography of our fall
but tells little or nothing   of much but beauty.

As such rubble is nothing   but symptoms or sultry
reminders we're flesh   that we ache above all.

As we have little   but the sultry gestures of lovers;
our outlines pressed   into patches of grass.

As the little we have   must be shared with others
or rationed   or sterilised by the glass.

As Hesiod said   to the girls from Pieria
we're haply destined   to love our destruction.

As faith is the condition   by which we sin
so I think of you   I wish you were here.

Epistle

Years away   or less   you do not know this song;
the way we drink to it   the stupefaction

of our dance   this girl who makes the air
gelatinous.   Your metaphors have changed;

your gut no longer turns   with her absence.
And no   our melodies are no more wedded

to the Phrygian   than are our hands content
kept clean of transgression.   Beyond this revelry

—   these riffs   that seem to hold the sun   in solstice   —
I   at least   am hopeless.   Beware the academics

who have read of us   and   might try to piece together
our revival   you'll find no masterworks

amongst our debris   this is not Pompeii
nor Ercolano   there are no signs of our times.

JAMES WOMACK

James Womack was born in Cambridge in 1979. He studied Russian and English Literature at university, and has lived in Russia, Iceland and Spain. He currently lives in Madrid where, together with his wife, the Spanish writer Marian Womack, he runs the publishing house Nevsky Prospects, which publishes Spanish translations of Russian literature. James has had poems published in several magazines, including *The Wolf*, *Areté* and *PN Review*, and has been shortlisted for a number of poetry prizes, including the Eric Gregory Award. His translation of Silvina Ocampo's *La torre sin fin* will be published by Hesperus. He is currently preparing an anthology of translations of young Spanish poets, and has completed a critical study of W.H. Auden and translation.

Intercuts

I *EXT: The Mouth of Hell*

A garden, as a child might build it,
Garden of bricks and blocky shrubbery:
By the fantastic urns and aristocratic hedges
Two figures: he and she.
(Intertitle: *'How did you come here?'*)
He wears a bedsheet-toga and sandals,
Plywood lyre propped on one arm.
This is the high pornography of 1907 –
She is naked, her hair undone.
(*'Come with me, come back home.'*)
The garden is poppies and thistles –
Would be grey in Technicolor.
She wants to offer her hand,

As he reaches for it, she withdraws.
(*'Do not look back. I will follow.'*)
His whiteface strains at sorrow, turns away
Back on the path he had taken.
What horrors have grown here?
The backcloth is painted shade and fingers.
(*'I do not hear you. I must turn! I must!'*)
And we do not see him turn,
Just a single shot of her in the garden.
A naked ghost, her dark eyes closed
And then, with a Méliès twist, she is gone.

II *INT: Her Flat*

Two hundred seconds of ancient celluloid
Threaded into the machine and thrown
In a square of light on their bedroom wall.
He winds the reel back, Eurydice
Doomed always to try again.
She wears the willow-pattern dressing gown
And her high copper hair drawn up.
Her legs across his lap, and his hand
Rests on them, at the top of the thigh.
The skin feels smooth – blue of the gown,
And the rain's blue light at the window.

III *M.O.S.*

(*'You can hear me, you can touch me.'*)
Surreptitiously, other people cut themselves
Into the film, and soon he is seeing them
As they shall be when they are the past.
Sweat sticks the hair to her forehead,
For one second he grasps her arm
And both recoil, for she has no skin
Just a ghost of flesh on a smooth white bone.
I will not go through with this, she says
And she was not there any more.
An unattained wife. He passes on
Through easily soluble mazes, old as core-ice,
Calls hopelessly Comrade to those he sees.
(*'I am not a shadow. I am not one of you.'*)

Dark and stormys

a.

What else should I do
but commemorate
meals and conversations?
It was a night
we drank dark and stormys
rum and lime and ginger ale
and Arima told me
about the end of the world
– an account so detailed
it must be true –
I've not seen her for years
she still writes
or wants to write

b.

And a year elsewhere
talking out again
in Reykjavík
– a bent-iron dormitory –
I made dark and stormys
as an inadequate
birthday present
ten of us in the kitchen
juicing limes
rum and ginger ale

Juan Bautista ran in
and called above our gabble
the lights! the aurora!
– all of us on the balcony
in the stairwell –
and the sky split open
a crack above our heads
with the green light dancing
nobody said a word
the light spread above us
to halve the world
This Arima said
this is how it starts

Seven Fragments

I

You never told me how boring it is to be mad
With you it was always gin and parties
And the solar radio that remembered
Its songs with the sunrise.

II

You were the bright shaman of St Petersburg
Who knew that visions only come
Through exhaustion, after the dancing
When you have changed your mind.

III

(And even enlightenment is precarious –
People can fall down stairs and break
The tiny mirrors in their eyes.)

IV

Moments of collapse,
When those enormous emotions
Absconded – you couldn't walk
And held my knees on the kitchen floor.
No longer alone, you felt tired –
Es ist richtig so Anna, aber so schwer.

V

Sure we were there
Eden unlost for a month or so
But no more than that, no more.

VI

And we promised to write, but knew we would not.

VII

Outside this window is an empty lawn
The wind embroiders
In silver-green liberty patterns.
    I wake with the fear that I have been
With one who was already dead –
And shuffle to the table
To gather my scattered drafts.

The True Scholar

When they come to write the novel of those years,
You will of course be a minor character,
Not having fucked your students,
Been an amusing drunk,
Or ridiculously addicted to Derrida.

So when M.S., in his soutane
And suntan, has discovered Rome
Or the T.M. affair is no more
Than a blistering memory
You will be where you have always been:

The coping-stone, happy as Pangur's monk
'Bringing difficulty to clearness'.
You will point out, scrupulously,
That this can be read both ways.

Young Romance

> *Look into her eyes and read the answer to the question...*
> *CAN ANY MAN BE TRUSTED?*

Let us leave for a moment the bukkake-faced virgin, Our Lady of
the pulp-magazine, and look instead into her sunglasses.

Although we are – are we? we are – in front of her, the lenses do
not reflect us, are no reflection of us, but show instead the same
image twice, two people, neither of them us, in a teenage embrace.

But maybe one of them is us, we are either the swooning twin
girls or else the pair of rugged heartbreakers, our hairy forearms
and manly hands possessing the shoulders of our new beloveds.

We shift position slightly between the lenses, our hands grip the
person we love more closely to our differently-ruffled shirts.

Three scars prod across our faces, or two scars: the light comes at different angles across our bright background.

We are green, we are green and captured inside our separate black eggs, and then inside their off-white and presumably plastic frames.

And these in their turn are where the watcher's eyes should be: we have replaced her eyes with our kisses and similarly clenched hands.

Her Monroe lips are parted and she has no front teeth, just a brilliant gumshield, and at the ends of her fingers two more little red eggs that reflect the light.

What do we stand before; what is behind us?

What causes these lines of black and whitewash to fall down the unreliable smooth face of her face?

What is coming from behind us?

Our background is also cut off, her purple scarf and henna bob filing the boundaries to our vision; even one of our eggs is divided, we can only imagine that it is whole beyond our limits, and that these curtailed but double satisfactions are a true picture, a true reflection of what we are.

Who knows if we can be trusted; who knows?

To the best of our knowledge we have told you what we see, and if these heroes and heroines are not us, then we have no place here.

Pathfinder

Leaving the bright town to the desert
Of three P.M. on a Sunday afternoon –
The immigrants sweeping down the hotel floors.
Half-full buckets, unlicensed cactus pear
On a dusty street corner, the heat of the day
And the lower slopes, past acres of hangdog sunflowers.

Snails cobbling the aloes.
Enough trees ahead to see no more than trees
Until you are at them, and they open.
You mount always, over the valley:
A mudslip has slid a *V* from the other hillside.
A moth closes sticky and tight to a sycamore seed.

Not trackless, there are too many paths
Through the shade, dead footsteps on the needles
The air claggy, a thin river runs past
Without stopping. Climb higher among the trees
Lean against any one for solid help.
And her bones were turned to branches.

The trees break and you half fall
Onto an overgrown and sunken avenue,
It curves along the contours and ends
Where you end, in gardens of the empty house.
Pass through the vacant rooms, the open windows,
You cannot lose yourself.

Dead, like they die in the theatre.
I imagine us here, on the sill of the big house
Talking under the lintel of a doorway
You do not invite me through. Time strolls in the garden,
A heavy crop of pears that rots down each year,
The espaliered fruit trees, herbs, all grown wild.